DEMOCRATIC ARCHITECTURE

DEMOCRATIC ARCHITECTURE

Practical Solutions
to Today's Housing Crisis

DONALD MacDONALD, F.A.I.A.

WHITNEY LIBRARY OF DESIGN
an imprint of Watson-Guptill Publications/New York

For Pia, Ian, and Denise

Acknowledgments

I would like to thank the following people for their help and support in the preparation of this book: Ivor Brown, Diana Dinkelacker, Marijke Gantvoort, Debra Harrington , Walt Harrington, Jim Heron, Liesbeth Heikens, Camden Hicks, Bill Hull, Jonathan Kanda, Gerd Kauschke, Richard Klein, Alex Kulakoff, Tom Lauderbach, Denise Lee, Dorena Lee, Lynette Lee, Denise MacDonald, Ian MacDonald, Sue MacDonald, Caspar Mol, Andrew Oliver, Ed Pearlstien, Mary Shu, Donald Turner.

Editor: Micaela Porta
Designer: Abigail Sturges
Production Manager: Hector Campbell

Published in 1996 by Whitney Library of Design, an imprint of Watson-Guptill Publications, a division of BPI Communications, Inc., 1515 Broadway, New York, NY 10036.

Cataloging-in-Publication Data is on file with the Library of Congress.

Manufactured in the United States
First printing, 1996
1 2 3 4 5 6 7 8 9 /02 01 00 99 98 97 96

CONTENTS

INTRODUCTION

All buildings built should serve the liberation of mankind, liberating the lives of individuals.

Frank Lloyd Wright

Because of the architectural profession's traditional devotion to designing monumental buildings and homes for the wealthy, it has paid very little attention to the housing needs of the great majority of the people. My proposals for democratic architecture in this book are intended to rectify that imbalance. They are based on four principles.

The first is that every human being has a right to a home—not just shelter but a private, secure, and congenial place to live at an affordable cost or, in the case of the destitute, no cost at all. Hundreds of thousands of people are wandering the streets of American cities because they have nowhere else to go. Countless more are huddled in squalid tenements, welfare hotels, shanties, and dilapidated housing projects. An estimated one-third of American households spend so much of their income for rent or mortgage payments that they have little left over for other necessities, including food in some instances.[1] Add to those figures the number of homeless and inadequately housed in other countries and the total is in the hundreds of millions.

Many of my proposals are practical designs for low- and lower-middle-income housing, with an emphasis on increasing opportunities for home ownership. They include a variety of detached homes, multiunit buildings, and some alternative types of housing for people whose lifestyles diverge from the mainstream. Most have been built and lived in; they are not dreams of what might be in a better world, but examples of what has been successfully tried, of what can be done to ultimately solve the housing crisis.

Second, the primary goal of residential design is to satisfy the needs and desires of the people who will live in a building. Except for the privileged few, people move into homes designed according to someone else's specifications and are then forced to adapt as best they can to the space and to other conditions beyond their power to change. This basic deprivation of freedom has existed for so long that it has never been seriously questioned. People should have as much control as possible over the design of their homes. They should be able to manipulate space and change details as they see fit. Therefore, some of my proposals provide ways to expand and divide houses, reshape the interiors, and even change the façades easily and relatively inexpensively.

Third, in deciding where and how to construct a building every effort must be made to prevent damage to the environment. In her classic analysis of urban planning, *The Death and Life of Great American Cities* published in the early 1960s, Jane Jacobs described the destructive environmental results of suburban sprawl, which at the time was just beginning: "Each day, several thousand more acres of our countryside are eaten by the bulldozers, covered by pavement . . . . Our irreplaceable heritage of Grade I agricultural land . . . is sacrificed for highways or supermarket parking lots as ruthlessly and unthinkingly as the trees in the woodlands are uprooted, the streams and rivers polluted, and the air itself filled with. . . gasoline exhausts."[2] Since then, of course, the blight has spread to the point that concrete, asphalt, and brick overlaid with ever-thickening smog radiate for miles from our cities, with hardly a tree or blade of grass left standing. My proposals include a number of alternatives to suburban sprawl.

Finally, design aesthetics should express the multiplicity of society, not some ideal of perfection or political ideology. This principle is an extension of Frank Lloyd Wright's assertion that "there should be as many kinds (styles) of houses as there are kinds (styles) of people and as many differentiations as there are different individuals." Wright's view was that a design should emerge organically, from "within outward," from the confluence of a building's functions and environment unfettered by preconceptions. Each building should be unique, integral, and harmonious, a true "entity," to use one of his favorite words. However, classical harmony—the design of symmetrical forms—does not represent the interplay of ideas, cultures, lifestyles, and aspirations that characterize a genuinely democratic society. Variety, dissonance, and the interplay between order and chaos within, as well as between, buildings do.

For architects, adherence to these principles requires a very different attitude from the commonly held one expressed by Philip Johnson when he said, "The job of an architect is to create beautiful buildings. That's all." That is not all, by any means. We architects also have a responsibility to do everything we can to create a more humane society. When there is want and suffering due to a lack of housing, we should apply our skills toward finding remedies. We may not have much say in the political decisions and financing policies that determine to a large extent whether or not homes actually get built, but we can exert professional leadership by showing what can be achieved.

Moreover, we should derive our creative inspiration from people, instead of abstruse theories of beauty or romantic notions about the spirit of the time. The inspiration should come from responding to unfulfilled needs, requiring a willingness to view people as individuals—not types—and life as it really is—not as we would like it to be. Designs are thus rooted in the variety of human experience. Only when they reflect heterogeneity, continuous change, and the dignity of the individual can they truly express the spirit of democracy.

DONALD MACDONALD
San Francisco, 1996

Chapter One

A HOME FOR EVERYONE

FAILURES IN PLANNING

Until the late 1970s the usual approach to providing low-income, and even some middle-income, housing was to build large institution-like projects, crowding in as many units as possible. The majority were concrete and steel boxes, benefiting little—if at all—from architectural amenities. Psychologist Robert Sommer described the mentality behind them:

> "In mental hospitals of the early 1950s [when many of the projects were built], the line was, 'If you give the patients anything nice, they won't take care of it.' For public housing tenants it went, 'If you provide good architecture, they won't appreciate it.' There is the same denigrating we/they dichotomy in all these assessments of people's response to their surroundings. We know what's best for them and they don't. Even if we provide what they say they'd like, they won't take care of it and will probably destroy it."[1]

Some projects, however, were designed by distinguished architects, among them Pruitt-Igoe in St. Louis by Minoru Yamasaki and Twin Parks Northeast in New York by Richard Meier and Partners. Pruitt-Igoe, drawing on the Swiss architect Le Corbusier's ideas for urban design, consisted of forty-three eleven-story buildings in a parklike setting. It won a national design award.

The high-rise Twin Parks Northeast was also acclaimed, in this case for the way it was integrated into a neighborhood of low-rise buildings. Today's supporters of contextualism would

Housing project, 500 Francisco Street, near Fisherman's Wharf in San Francisco. Over the years the housing area has become a center where many criminals prey on the tourists who frequent Fisherman's Wharf. When this project was designed it won awards, just like the Pruitt-Igoe project that was finally demolished in St. Louis, Missouri.

Aerial view of Pruitt-Igoe project in St. Louis, circa 1957. The small and varied scale of the surrounding residential properties was overlooked by the bureaucrats and architects who planned Pruitt-Igoe. Their attitude was typical of this period of U.S. history.

find the claim farfetched. The project's integration depended on its blending into the city street grid pattern by way of the modular spacing of the high-rise solids and voids.

Neither project won any praise from its tenants, however. People refused to live in Pruitt-Igoe because of vandalism and serious crime, and in 1972, just fifteen years after it was completed, the city of St. Louis dynamited the project.

Twin Parks Northeast also failed miserably. Within a few years after it opened in 1973, many of its 523 apartments had been vacated, indeed some were burned out. A report about what went wrong cited specific design and construction deficiencies, vandalism, and inadequate maintenance—which was precisely what could be said about most of the low-income projects built after World War II. But the underlying problem at virtually all of them, whether architecturally graced or not, was the pervasive paternalism of the people who developed the projects: We know what is best for the tenants and they do not.

As it turned out, the government agencies, planners, and designers did not know what was best or even passably good. What did Le Corbusier's ideas about urban design and Meier's about contextualism have to do with the daily lives of the people for whom the projects were built? What did the other impersonal,

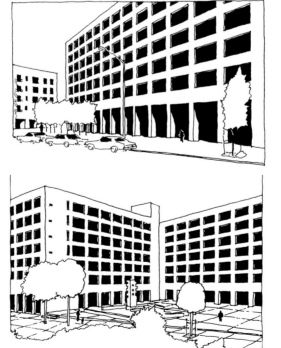

Two views of Richard Meier's Twin Parks Northeast project. The illustration shows the lack of small design elements of residential scale needed to individualize the exterior walls. This unpleasantly austere look would probably have been avoided had there been community participation in the initial stages of the design process.

often ugly, steel-and-concrete slabs have to do with the wishes or desires of the people who lived in them? No wonder the projects were vandalized and crime-ridden. Their "scale, scope, and impermeability," as Sommer put it, were "oppressive to the human spirit."[2] Treat people inhumanely, and they are apt to respond in kind. The deterioration of projects nationwide became so serious that many cities followed the example of St. Louis and tore a number of the projects down.

Because of the calamitous fate of such housing projects, there has been a revival of interest among planners and government agencies in the mass-produced Levittown houses built for middle-income families after World War II. However, the informing mentality behind Levittown differed little from that of the projects. The developer Levitt and Sons built the first Levittown (as the communities were named) in 1947; it consisted of 17,000 identical Cape Cod–style single-family houses side by side row after row on a 1400-acre site in a suburb of New York City. The concept was to minimize costs by placing "the machine in the service of the hearth." Virtually every component of the house, from the lumber to the nails, was standardized and manufactured in large quantities to the developer's exact specifications. Trucks delivered bundles of materials to each site, and the construction workers and machinery moved from site to site performing exactly the same operations. It was the assembly line applied to housing construction. For its second development, this one in Bucks County, Pennsylvania, the firm intended to elaborate the concept into a planned community of neighborhoods replete with parks, playgrounds, and schools. Things did not quite work out that way because of political problems, but they did work in the third Levittown, which was built in New Jersey in the 1960s.

Similar planned communities were built in the 1950s and 1960s by other large developers outside major cities throughout the country. In northern California, the usual type of house was the "stucco box," so called because the stucco walls were left flat and blank, with no architectural detailing other than pastel-colored paint. It was a chintzy version of the International Style. Some of the communities were less rigidly designed than the Levittowns: curved streets instead of the strict grid pattern, some differences in size, and a little variety in the basic Cape Cod, ranch, or other style of the homes. (In fact, the New Jersey Levittown also varied the designs and street layouts.)

Nevertheless, every community was homogeneous. Essentially, they were horizontal versions of middle-income housing

Aerial view of a section of Levittown, Long Island, first of the three Levittowns which were built between 1947 and the mid-1960s. Note the lack of landscaping and the poor integration of the drainage reservoir into the site plan.

Stucco box project in Daly City, California. The simple detached homes in the foreground are virtually identical with each other except for the modest façades which have evolved over the years. The houses sited on the hill above are all the same.

projects. And not only the architecture was homogeneous. All the residents of a community earned more or less the same income, shared similar values, and (until enactment of the civil rights laws of the 1960s) were white and in some instances of the same ethnic background. The historian Daniel J. Boorstin pointed out the paternalistic nature of the communities:

> In large developments where the developer had a plan, and even in the smaller developments, there was a new kind of paternalism: not the quasi-feudal paternalism of the company town, nor the paternalism of the utopian ideologue. This new kind of paternalism was fostered by the American genius for organization, by the rising twentieth-century American standard of living, and by the American genius for mass production. It was the paternalism of the marketplace. The suburban developer, unlike the small-town booster, seldom intended to live in the community he was building. For him community was a commodity, a product to be sold at a profit. And the suburban homeowner often moved into a whole town which had been shaped in advance by a shrewd developer's sense of the market.[3]

It can be said for the developers that at least they got relatively inexpensive houses built at a time when people were desperate to buy them, and since the early 1980s their example has been the basis for a new approach to the housing shortage in urban areas. Emphasis has been placed on small dwellings priced to enable people with modest incomes to buy them.

One such development began in 1982 with the Nehiamiah Houses in Brooklyn, which consisted of street after street of two-

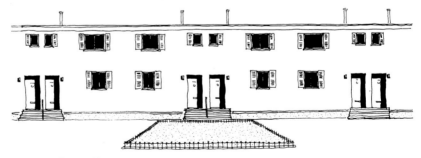

Exterior Elevation

Exterior front elevation and typical street layout of Nehiamiah Houses in Brooklyn, New York. Note the lack of individually designed facades needed to create an identity for each unit.

Site Plan

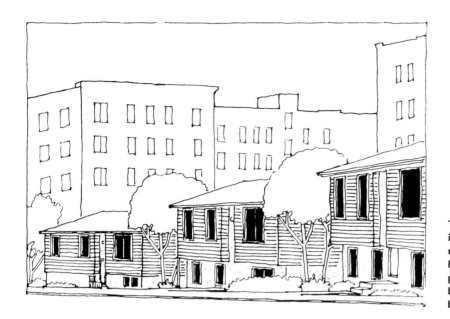

Typical street scene showing Charlotte Gardens' new detached, prefabricated houses. Behind this new project are silhouetted burned-out apartment buildings.

story row houses. Eighteen feet wide and fifty-five feet deep with brick facades, the houses were—in the words of the architectural historian Richard Plunz—"reminiscent of nineteenth-century mill housing. The only significant difference is the setback from the street, which serves as parking for the family automobile. . . . The relationship between Nehiamiah Houses and the nineteenth-century goes beyond appearance. The houses hearken back to Gilded Age private philanthropy for the 'deserving poor'. . . upwardly mobile families whose advanced status is rewarded with superior housing at reduced cost." While much of the site had already been cleared for urban renewal, a number of buildings in good condition were razed for the project on the dubious grounds of cost efficiency. One of the people who would be displaced remarked angrily:

> Now they're talking about building a one-family house out of inferior materials and putting my family in there, putting two families in a one-family house. The Nehiamiah plan started off by saying, we want to build on empty lots. Now they went from building on empty lots to now taking this man's furniture store, acquiring our grocery store. Where will we have the shops? Where will we go? Where will my father go? He has finished paying for the house, now they want him to pay for another mortgage.

Another project, the Charlotte Gardens, begun at the same time as the Nehiamiah Houses but located in the Bronx in the shadow of some burned-out apartment buildings, consisted of prefabricated houses with a house-trailer type of construction. Plunz compares it with the early Levittown. Commenting on the development, he says, "Charlotte Gardens is another variant on the philanthropy of the Gilded Age. It is not housing for the poor in the same sense that public housing programs were, with their legally enforced policy of open admissions for any family that needed housing, regardless of economic circumstance or social problems. Like Nehiamiah, Charlotte Gardens represents an opportunity only for the 'deserving poor,' which is to say the lower middle class, with the economic and social wherewithal for assimilation into the myths and privileges of cottage ownership."[4]

Although the Nehiamiah and Charlotte Gardens developments have one positive aspect—they offer separate houses and ownership for people who want them—they exemplify the disdain and authoritarian imposition of conformity that have generally characterized housing for all but the well-to-do or fortunate. The houses are more containers than homes. A true home has three qualities: It must afford the occupants as much individual privacy as possible, it must offer a reasonable sense of security, and above all, the dwelling must be congenial, agreeable to one's outlook on life.

Of privacy, the environmental psychologist Robert Gifford has said that it is "an important part of the individual's sense of self or identity." He goes on to discuss privacy in relation to housing:

> A residence is already a relatively private space. In the developed world, the walls and doors provided by our houses are probably the commonest mechanisms we actually use to manage privacy, even though some surveys report that many individuals associate residential privacy with exterior factors, such as lot size and distance from neighbors . . . within the house, different levels of privacy are needed for different family members. Of course, if a house is very large, privacy is not a problem unless it is so large that family members become isolated and alienated from one another. More often, unfortunately, the problem is insufficient space or poor arrangement of the available space. . . . Outside the residence itself, privacy may vary as a function of design in multi-unit housing projects. [D.P.] McCarthy and [S.] Saegert studied privacy in the lobbies, elevators, and other public areas within low-rise and high-rise buildings. Naturally, such areas offer less privacy than a person's own apartment, but McCarthy and Saegert found that public areas in low-rise design were judged by residents to offer more privacy than public areas in the high-rise design. . . . Clearly, there is no universal design for residential privacy. Each family or client's needs must be carefully considered if the designer is to provide a cost-efficient yet private dwelling. However, some groups are sufficiently similar that some design considerations may apply to most buildings serving them.[5]

The second requisite attribute is security. Because of the growing crime rate, sociologists, psychologists, and, of course, criminologists have studied the problem of security intensively. What they have generally found is that strong locks and barred windows do not assure safety. More important is what architect and urban designer Oscar Newman calls "defensible space design" of the housing environment "by grouping dwelling units to reinforce associations of mutual benefit; by delineating paths of movement; by defining areas of activity for particular users through their juxtaposition with internal living areas; and by providing for natural opportunities for visual surveillance."[6] Newman was referring to multiunit buildings, particularly housing projects, but the principle also applies to private houses.

Privacy and security are not enough to make a dwelling democratic, however. In addition to meeting physical needs, housing must suit a person's or family's cultural outlook, social relationships, habits, and idiosyncrasies as much as possible. The attribute of congeniality is the crux of democratic architecture. It means respect for individuality, for the right of self-expression and self-determination.

INDIVIDUALIZING DESIGN

While the ideal would be to build each home in accordance with the specific needs of the people who will live in it, the fact is that we rarely know beforehand who that will be and, of course, there are also economic constraints. Consequently, the basic designs have to meet categories of needs within a range of budgets. Middle-income couples with children, low-income single-parent families, the infirm elderly, alcoholic vagrants, adventurous wanderers, the self-employed working at home, upper-income executives, craftsmen who want their workshops in their homes, and so on require different designs, which might have to be modified to accommodate ethnic preferences. The first step in the design process therefore is to conduct interviews and study whatever one can find to determine what the people who fit the category want—a procedure that would be anathema to the "create beautiful buildings" architects and too much trouble for many others. Interviewing can be difficult. Finding the people concerned and getting appointments is time-consuming. Some people are inarticulate. Others are wary of anyone who appears to represent authority or is condescending, which architects tend to be. In

Exterior Elevation

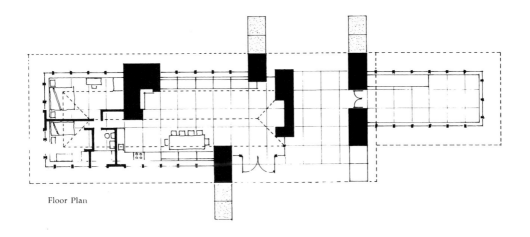

Floor Plan

Typical front exterior elevation and ground floor
plan of Wright's Usonian
Automatic House. On the
plan the four-foot grid is
set up for the block mod-
ule. The homemade con-
crete block of a standardized form is used for the
wall and roof structure,
thereby simplifying the
number and complexity of
component parts needed
for the house construction.

Construction of a home-
made masonry unit. The
formwork shown is con-
structed of wood boards,
although it could also be
constructed of sheet
metal. The knock-out
panel allows the remaining
block shape to be used as
a structural roof element
or lintel.

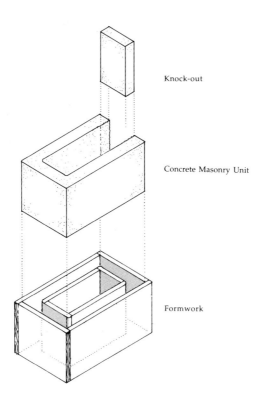

Knock-out

Concrete Masonry Unit

Formwork

addition, a lot of explanation might be required. People often know very little, if anything, about codes, construction methods, and budgets, not to mention basic architecture. The whole process involves mutual education, and for the architect it can be an invaluable source of inspiration.

A design concept that meets a group's fundamental needs does not necessarily satisfy the individual members of the group. To individualize a building, the design should enable people to make adjustments themselves. Frank Lloyd Wright developed one way in his "build-it-yourself" Usonian Automatic Houses. The basic structural element of the house was a homemade concrete block. Anybody with rudimentary skill and a great deal of patience could make a mold out of sheet metal or wood, pour in concrete to form the blocks, then fit them together with light metal rods to build the walls, upper floors, and roof. Other basic elements consisted of a simple concrete slab for a combined foundation and floor, and bathrooms and kitchens easily assembled from mass-produced products. As Wright said, "Here then, within moderate means for the free man of our democracy, with some intelligence and by his own energy, comes a . . . house that may be put to work in our society [to] give us an architecture for 'housing' which is becoming to a free society because, though standardized fully, it yet establishes the democratic ideal of variety—the sovereignty of the individual."[7]

While the build-it-yourself concept is attractive in many respects, it is impractical for people who have to work eight hours a day, and in any event the concrete blocks proved very difficult for amateurs to handle. However, the idea of a more or less standardized unit with the capability of "do-it-yourself" changes, or having someone else do them for you, is practical. Many houses are built with unfinished attics or basements to permit the creation of new rooms. But there are other ways, too, even in apartments, to allow for modifications, and the capability should be a fundamental design element. Privately owned houses should also permit simple external modification to suit the owners' taste and, if site conditions allow, expansion to meet changing needs.

ENVIRONMENTAL IMPACT

Almost as important as the design of housing is the question of where it will be built. We can no longer ignore the environmental damage caused by expansion into undeveloped suburban areas.

Jane Jacobs' solution was to halt the flight to suburbia by developing our cities and making them attractive and stimulating places to live.

A study done by the Real Estate Research Corporation on the economic and environmental impact of new residential development provides strong support for her conclusion. Results of the study indicate that high-density housing of the type found in urban areas is considerably less expensive from both an economic and environmental point of view than suburban sprawl, traditionally characterized by block after block of single-family homes lined up in the conventional grid pattern. The purpose of the study was "to help the mayor, the city manager, the planning board, and other concerned local officials" answer such questions as whether the added tax base provided by residential growth would offset the costs to the community and what were the effects of development on air and water pollution, wildlife, open space, energy and water consumption, and the lives of the new residents and their neighbors.[8] To every question the answer was that high density is better. For example:

- Costs for roads and utilities are about fifty-five percent lower. Therefore, local governments save money to the extent that they bear financial responsibility for the installation of infrastructure. Operating and maintenance costs are also lower. In addition, there is less need for public transportation.
- Only about half as much land is required. So the potential for preserving open space, with the trees still standing and the grass still growing, is much higher.
- Air pollution from heating and automobiles is about half, with most of the reduction coming from the fact that residents do not have to drive as far.
- Pollution from storm water and sediment is less, because the total paved area is smaller.
- Energy consumption is less because of the reduced use of autos and public transportation.
- Fewer traffic accidents occur.

The answer to continued sprawl is to confine new construction as much as possible to developed urban and suburban areas. In most communities there is plenty of space available—vacant lots too small for the usual housing or commercial building but quite suitable for one or more cottage-type homes; border areas between commercial and residential zones that are excellent for mixed-use development (as are many other areas); air rights over developed property, roads, and utilities; and even backyards that can accommodate small houses.

But infill can, and very often does, provoke furious resistance, particularly in the more prosperous neighborhoods, where the thought of introducing low-income or even middle-income homes or stores raises the specters of plunging property values and an undesirable mix of different ethnic groups and classes. Very often the specters are just that—phantoms born of irrational fears. Whether they are or not, true democracy involves an intermingling of people without regard for their class or color or work, and I venture to say that if there were more such mingling many of the fears and social problems would disappear.

AFFORDABILITY

The central issue, of course, is how to reduce the cost of housing, and that requires a thorough reexamination of long-cherished ideas about housing standards. The first requisite change is in the traditional concept of livable space. Over the years, the notion has developed that a certain amount of space has to be allotted for each person and for each activity. In the United States, it has been generally accepted as gospel that there must be an eight-foot-high bedroom for every two people (because precut lumber studs are eight feet long). A middle-class mythology of space has emerged. The assumption is that what people would like to have is what they have to have, whether or not they can afford it. As a result, a great many people have no space at all.

The cost of housing can be substantially reduced if that way of thinking is reversed. A design of affordable housing should not start with the question of how to build least expensively to meet certain space requirements, but what is the maximum amount of space that can be provided for someone who can pay a certain rent or mortgage. If it means lowering the ceiling and reducing the size of the bedroom to meet the budget, that has to be done. A 7-foot, or even 6.5-foot, ceiling is ample as long as there is adequate ventilation. A sixty-four-foot-square bedroom will easily accommodate a double bed and a dresser.

In fact, bedrooms in the traditional sense can be eliminated entirely, or the number reduced, if we get away from the idea that space has to be assigned a function. As everyone who has lived in a studio apartment knows, a living room can be turned into a bedroom easily enough. Extend the concept to what would ordinarily be a multiroom unit occupied by a family with children. With a series of partitions, a single room can be used as living space during the day and divided into bedrooms at night—or divided whenever needed for the sake of privacy. The same principle can be applied to a small house or one floor of a two-story house. For a family it provides considerable flexibility, an instant guest room, additional bedrooms as the family grows, rooms of different sizes for children of different ages, or an area that can be a so-called family room during the day and bedrooms at night.

In addition, order and common sense have to be brought to the labyrinth of codes that make it very difficult, if not impossible, to build low-cost housing. On the surface, and viewed individually, many of the code provisions appear to be justified. Who would argue that we should not conserve energy, prevent fire damage, reduce health hazards, and ensure the structural safety of buildings under a wide range of loads? But when we balance risks and costs, when we consider ideals of security in terms of the urgent need for housing, what are the priorities?

For example, do we always have to have double walls with insulation and double-glazed windows to save energy, even in a moderate climate like California's? Under what conditions are fire sprinklers and one-hour fire-resistant walls necessary even though they greatly increase the cost of construction? Which is more important to health: a hallway between the bathroom and the kitchen or not having a bathroom or kitchen at all? Must all stairways be designed in the expectation that they will be climbed by people with heart conditions, despite the fact that to do so costs more because of the required space? What are reasonable fiber-stress requirements in wood construction, based on sound engineering for realistic loads, not on what the lumber interests say? Moreover, for every code there is a different regulatory agency, for every agency there are different procedures, for each procedure there are stipulations and modifications, and on top of all this there are planning departments and review boards and special interest groups.

The objection often raised to code modifications is that in paring the codes the poor receive inferior housing, that they are deprived of the comfort and safety enjoyed by the wealthy, and that injustice is being perpetuated. But is that really the point of view of the people who are homeless, or of families who are forced to share apartments with relatives, or of young couples who cannot afford to buy a house? Safety and space are measured by needs, not by abstract theories. Legitimate concerns about energy, fire, structural integrity, and health are one thing, but standards developed essentially for upper-middle-income homes require serious reevaluation.

AESTHETICS

✗ good

Questions are also inevitably raised about the aesthetics of buildings designed to respond to individual needs and to reduce costs. Won't that mean a hodgepodge of shapes, colors, and ornamentation, as well as some ugly boxes? Regarding the hodgepodge, the answer is hopefully yes; about boxes, the answer is no, provided architects respond creatively to human needs and stop boxing themselves in by ideologies and mannerisms. If one design characteristic can be said to be most expressive of democracy, it is fragmentation. In a true democracy, the diversity of people and goals, economic individualism, social and physical mobility, and variety of organizational structures defy the orderliness and consistency that have been the traditional objectives of architectural design. More appropriate objectives are disharmony, contradiction, flux, and disparity. They can be represented among buildings and within buildings by the introduction of a variety of forms, spatial relationships, and materials to achieve purposeful chaos within the order imposed by functional, economic, and environmental constraints. For the architect, acceptance of fragmentation as an objective of design can be an exalting creative experience. It liberates, allowing a natural flow of ideas, particularly in the vital initial stages of design. But the approach takes courage and strength. The architect has to reject easy, tried solutions to problems. He has to take chances and be prepared to fail.

Fragmentation, however, does not mean disorder and originality for their own sake. Its purpose is to satisfy the functional and aesthetic needs of the people who inhabit buildings, not to be a realization of the architect's subjective impulses. Although a creative architect undoubtedly commences the design process by unleashing his imagination, his ultimate success will depend on how well he harnesses his freewheeling thoughts to the requirements of the people he is serving. I want to emphasize the word *serving* here, because that is what we architects do and always have done. We place our artistry at the disposal of clients. Historically, we have served monarchs, priests, oligarchs, and—more recently—tycoons. The purpose of this book is to show how we can serve the people.

Chapter Two

HOME SPACE

The most exact definition of architecture that can be given today is that which takes into account interior space. . . . That space—void—should be the protagonist of architecture is after all natural. Architecture is not art alone, it is merely a reflection of conceptions of life or a portrait of systems of living. Architecture is environment, the stage on which our lives unfold.

Bruno Zevi[1]

HOW MUCH IS ENOUGH?

In his tale "How Much Land Does a Man Need?" Leo Tolstoy tells the story of a Russian peasant named Pakhom who had too little land to meet his needs, so he borrowed and otherwise scraped enough money together to buy forty acres. But Pakhom was still "too cramped to be comfortable," and learning of opportunities beyond the Volga he sold his property and moved with his family to a large village in the Volga Valley, where he acquired 125 acres of communal land in different fields. At first the peasant was happy with what he had, but soon came to the conclusion that he still did not have enough to sow wheat, which was what he wanted to do. Hearing that in the Bashkirs virgin soil could be bought for pennies an acre, he traveled to Bashkiria to find out if it was true. The Bashkirs turned out to be herders who lived in tents, had no interest in tillage, and though ignorant, were "good-natured enough." They agreed to sell Pakhom the land for "one thousand rubles a day." That is, for one thousand rubles he could have as much land as he could walk around in the course of the day, starting at sunrise and returning to the spot where he started by sunset. But if he failed to reach that spot before the sun went down he would forfeit one thousand rubles. Pakhom reached the spot on time, but in the race to do so suffered a heart attack and died. "His servant picked up the spade and dug a grave long enough for Pakhom to lie in, and buried him in it," writes Tolstoy. "Six feet from his head to his heels was all he needed."

Certain similarities exist between Tolstoy's cautionary tale and our current housing problem. How much space does a person need? And when the need and aspirations grow, how is more space to be obtained without destroying oneself financially in the attempt?

Le Corbusier satisfied himself "to the point of certainty that a human cell of fourteen square meters [about 151 square feet] per inhabitant could provide a basis of calculations that would lead to the expansion and flowering of men's lives in a machine age."[2] With the fourteen centares per person as a basic housing unit, he designed apartments for working-class families of various sizes, beginning with a living room, toilet with washbasin, and kitchen for a bachelor (fourteen square meters), and proceeded to multiply the allotted space by the number of people in the family. But as he himself admitted about the apartments, "The one person who won't want to live in them *is the worker!* [The italics are his.] He has not been educated, he is not ready to live in such apartments." As a solution to the worker's reluctance, he called for "the necessary paternal concern that would allow us *to enforce, to guide, to instruct.*"[3] (Again, the italics are his.) Later he improved upon the basic unit by reducing it to ten square meters—about 108 square feet—dimensions which Soviet architects used when adopting his concept for the construction of workers' housing in Moscow and other cities during the Khrushchev era.

Ingenious as the designs were, they stemmed from Corbusier's preoccupation with positing fundamental rules for architectural design and, indeed, all art. "Systematization brings liberty by means of order. And with order, poetry."[4]

In democratic architecture, there are no such rules, no preconceived and inflexible notions of how much space a worker or anybody else needs or should have, and certainly no attempt to bring liberty by means of order. The goal is to provide people with a private, secure, and congenial place to live at an affordable cost. That means creating space that they can control and dominate, instead of being dominated by it. Unlike the peasant

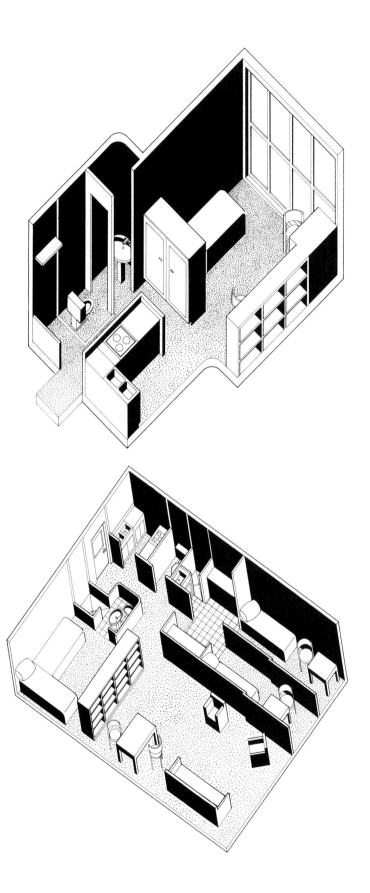

The Swiss-born architect Charles-Edouard Jeanneret (better known by his pseudonym Le Corbusier) designed a one-room bachelor apartment on the basis of his calculation of fourteen square meters—about 151 square feet—of floor space for each occupant of working-class housing. The apartment contained a living room, a kitchen, and a washbasin and toilet. Assuming that the building would have central air-conditioning, he specified air-tight plate glass for the façade.

Le Corbusier's apartment for a working-class family. Based on the fourteen-square-meter "biological unit" as he called it, Le Corbusier designed an apartment for a family of four with fifty-six square meters (about 603 square feet) of floor space. It contained a living room, a master bedroom, two bedrooms (for two children of different sexes or three or four children, depending on their gender), a kitchen, two bathrooms with showers, and a water closet. He also designed apartments for larger families, always in multiples of fourteen square meters per occupant. Le Corbusier admitted that workers would not want to live in the apartments and would have to be educated and forced to accept them.

Pakhom, they should not have to keep looking elsewhere and moving on to obtain more space as their needs increase and fortunes wax. A home should be alive; it should grow and change, and as it matures, gain a distinct personality.

MINIMIZING COSTS

In designing affordable housing, the major problem is how to minimize the cost of meeting certain criteria for livable space as much as possible. The criteria have been summarized in a "Design for Housing Checklist" developed by the American Institute of Architects Foundation:

APPROPRIATE ROOM SIZE, SHAPE, SCALE. Do the rooms have a pleasant feeling? Are the ceiling heights appropriate to room size?

EASE OF CIRCULATION. Are the rooms located conveniently to one another? Does the circulation path interfere with furniture layout?

ACCOMMODATION OF FURNISHINGS. Have rooms been designed with uses in mind? Does the kitchen have adequate work and storage areas?

VISUAL PRIVACY. Is there a sense of privacy between various rooms? Does the design consider a division between public and private areas? Should it?

ACOUSTICAL PRIVACY. Does the construction inhibit noise transfer between rooms?

ACCESSIBILITY FOR ELDERLY/HANDICAPPED. Can the various spaces be used by an elderly person or one who is wheelchair-bound?

NATURAL/ARTIFICIAL LIGHTING QUALITY. Does the design take advantage of daylighting? Has consideration been given to pleasant artificial lighting for nighttime use?

NATURAL VENTILATION. Is there cross-ventilation in the unit?

ADEQUACY OF INDOOR STORAGE. Has consideration been given to the amount and kinds of things residents might own and where these things should be stored?

APPROPRIATENESS OF FINISHES AND MATERIALS. Have materials been chosen for their ability to add to the quality of the environment? Are materials durable?

PLEASING DESIGN DETAILS. Are there special visual features or finishing touches? Has a sense of individuality been established?

INTEGRATION/ADEQUACY OF BUILDING SYSTEMS. Has attention been given to the way in which the heating, cooling, electrical, and plumbing systems affect the design/function/comfort of rooms?

OVERALL IMPRESSIONS. Does the unit feel like a home? Is this layout flexible in anticipation of changing resident needs?

Cottage-type houses can be much less expensive to build per unit and far more commodious than apartment buildings like those designed by Le Corbusier and his many followers. The basic design is for a two-story 20- x 20-foot detached house with a garden and on-site parking. Construction costs are minimized through such measures as use of the box shape, wood frame, and plywood siding, and installation of standard doors and windows. A combined living room/dining area/kitchen is placed upstairs under a high-pitched ceiling with skylights to provide a feeling of spaciousness. Some versions have a loft that can be converted into a bedroom. Downstairs are two bedrooms, or one bedroom and a garage, a bathroom, a back-yard, and a small front lawn. A parking space is provided in front of the two-bed-room house. So that the occupants can individualize their home, the cottage is con-ceived as an armature. Bay windows, decks, and even rooms can be added simply by bolting them onto the wood frame. The cottages shown here, located in San Francisco, were the first four built.

That most of the criteria can be met very satisfactorily in affordable housing is demonstrated by a group of cottages designed and built for sale or rent in a lower-middle-class neigh-borhood in San Francisco. The design became the prototype for a number of other cottages built in the San Francisco Bay area, with variations depending on the site, context, and other consid-erations. It also proved to be eminently applicable in the design of multiunit buildings, including a public housing project.

The design resulted from an experiment born of the desper-ate need in San Francisco (and, of course, elsewhere) for reason-ably priced housing. For the experiment, a 4800-square-foot lot was purchased in a transitional area, one characterized by run-down old Victorian homes that had been turned into multiunit dwellings. Some were being restored to their former grandeur, so the outlook for the neighborhood was promising. The lot was chosen partly because of its relatively low price—it had become a kind of neighborhood garbage dump—but also because construction on it would contribute to the redevelopment of the neighborhood and the property would therefore increase in value.

The lot was zoned for six units, and the total construction budget was based on the sale or rental of a unit for a monthly mortgage payment (or rent) that would be about the same as prevailing rents in the neighborhood, which were modest compared with many other areas of the city.

It quickly became evident that six units could not be built on the site within the budget. San Francisco's on-site parking requirements would necessitate construction of a three-story building. When the costs of labor, materials, elevator, fire escapes, and sprinklers were added up, it was impossible to meet the pricing criterion for the units. The building could be no more than two stories high.

From the attempts to figure out a way to fit six units into a two-story building without sacrificing quality, an amazing fact emerged. Instead of a multiple dwelling with a total of 4800 square feet of space, four detached two-story houses with about 800 square feet each plus yard could be built on the site at a cost low enough to yield just about as much profit as the originally projected six units. They would be small, but that was not necessarily a liability. At one time a great many of the homes in California—

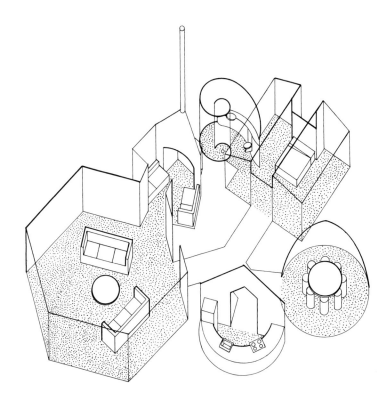

The design of the San Francisco cottage prototype began with a study of how much space was needed for such functions as talking with guests in the living room (left) or sitting around the fireplace (upper left), taking a shower (upper right), sleeping (right), eating (lower right), and cooking (bottom center).

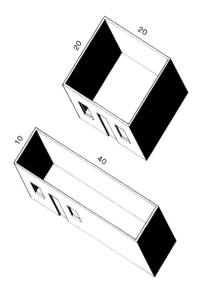

One method of minimizing construction costs was to adopt a square layout for the house. A 20- x 20-foot shape equals eighty linear feet of exterior wall, whereas a rectangular 40 x 10 feet, for example, adds up to 100 linear feet. The square shape has the additional advantage of requiring less seismic reinforcement, because it is more static.

perhaps most—were cottages or bungalows, and those that still existed in San Francisco in the 1980s were in great demand. For young men and women who were closed out of the housing market by the Bay Area's high prices, the cottages could provide opportunities for realizing the American dream of home ownership.

The design objective was to make the houses as commodious and attractive as possible within the same construction budget and with the same pricing criterion—that is, essentially, to minimize construction costs so that the occupants could have as much space and comfort as the budget would allow.

The design process began with a study of how much space was needed for certain functions—sleeping, cooking and eating, sitting around and talking or watching television, kids' playing, and so on, including the necessary furniture and fixtures. As Bruno Zevi put it, the study was "architecture without buildings." The idea was, again in his words, to adapt "spaces to human functions and movements."[5] It turned out that, given the 800 square feet of space in two stories, there was ample room for two bedrooms or one bedroom and a garage plus living room, kitchen, and bath. Two bedrooms were decided upon for three of the units, because that would make the house suitable for a couple with two young children or an older one, or for two singles. Yard space in front of those houses would have to be shared with an on-site parking area in accordance with San Francisco code requirements.

For economic and other reasons, a number of restrictions were placed on the design. First, the house was to be square. It was a matter of arithmetic. A 20- x 20-foot structure adds up to

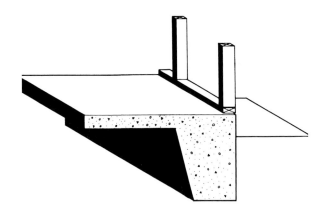

Another measure taken to minimize construction costs was the specification, where feasible, of a slab on grade with a perimeter footing for the foundation (right). This configuration is quite satisfactory for many types of soil. However, for cottages that were to be built on fill or hillsides, a grade beam and pier footing were selected. A proposal for building cottages in Russia specified a T footing, which goes below the frost line to prevent frozen pipes and soil upheaval.

80 linear feet of exterior wall, whereas a rectangular layout of, say, 40 x 10 feet comes out to 100 linear feet. While the savings in materials for one cottage are relatively small, they become substantial as the number of units increases. In addition, a square affords better resistance to earthquake forces, a very important consideration in California. A square building is more static than a rectangular one and therefore requires less seismic reinforcement—a further savings.

Second, the foundation had to be a slab on grade with a perimeter footing. The economy of eliminating a cellar is obvious. But the footing is also important, because the perimeter type is less expensive than a pile with a slab on grade. Certain site conditions would require the use of a more expensive T-type footing, which may include a retaining wall.

From various points of view, the most important requirement was a wood frame for the house. Wood affords many advantages. Construction with timber is much less expensive than construction using concrete or steel because it involves very few factory-produced elements, and many workers have the ability to build a wood frame, whereas concrete and steel require considerable skill and specialized equipment. Moreover, utility systems can be installed after the framing is complete simply by drilling through the wood wherever necessary. With concrete and steel, a great deal of time has to be spent on planning the installation, and special tools are needed if the frame is already in place. Another advantage of wood frames over other structural materials was proved dramatically during the severe earthquake that struck the San Francisco area in 1989. The wood was resilient. It absorbed shock, whereas concrete ruptured and steel vibrated and oscillated.

Further economy was achieved by using lumber no larger than 2 x 6 inches for the frame because as the size increases, the cost goes up geometrically. A 2- x 12-inch board is more than twice as expensive as a 2 x 6. (Actual sizes are often smaller; a 2 x 6 is usually 1.5 x 5.5, and a 2 x 4 is usually 1.5 x 3.5.

Another advantage of the small size is the weight—one person can hoist the boards easily, which can save on labor costs. The expense of labor was also minimized by the use of cross members instead of joint hangers for the frame to cut down on the amount of time-consuming craft work. Glue-laminated members were not used either because the cost of the manufactured products outweighed the price of the extra timber used in their place. However, the exterior of the house, the "skin," was to be made of structural-grade Douglas-fir plywood, which is not only economical but is also a good diaphragm, tying floors and walls together.

A long-term consideration in the specification of wood for the frame and skin was that the owner of the cottage should be able to make repairs and changes with a few basic tools obtainable at the local hardware store. Wood is a democratic building material. Almost anyone who has a little skill and patience can work with it. Witness the log cabins and Cape Cod cottages built by the American settlers, and the mail-order houses designed for amateur builders[6]—and Thoreau's cabin at Walden Pond:

> At length, in the beginning of May, with the help of some of my acquaintances,[7] rather to improve so good an occasion for neighborliness, than from any necessity, I set up the frame of my house.

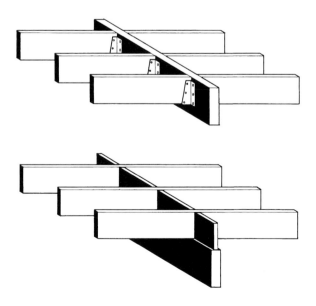

Among the ways labor costs were kept down was the use of cross members instead of hanging joists. In the latter type (top), each joist is attached to the bottom beam with a metal fastener. In a cross member (bottom), the joist is simply laid over the beam and held in place by wood blocks. The use of small boards for the frame also helped to minimize labor costs because the boards could be hoisted easily by one person.

. . . I began to occupy my house on the 4th of July, as soon as it was boarded and roofed, for the boards were carefully feather-edged and lapped, so that it was perfectly impervious to rain; . . . Before winter I built a chimney, and shingled the sides of my house, which were already impervious to rain, with imperfect and sappy shingles made of the first slice of the log, whose edges I was obliged to straighten with a plane. I have thus a tight shingled and plastered house, ten feet wide by fifteen long, and eight-feet posts, with a garret and a closet, a large window on each side, two trap doors, one door at the end, and a brick fireplace opposite.[8]

Granted that the tradition of the self-sufficient settler has not been passed on to our generation and that people who work eight hours a day do not have the time to build their own homes. But if they have the economic or creative incentive, the wood and the information on how to use it are readily available. As author Philip Langdon pointed out, "Years of testing have enabled lumber to emerge as something that construction specialists like to call 'an engineered material' with a known strength. A builder today who wants to span a certain distance, with wood that will carry an anticipated defined load, can turn to a species-specific chart and find, for instance, that 2 x 4's of kiln-fried Southern pine #2, placed every two feet, will safely span fourteen feet and carry a live load of forty pounds per square foot."[9] The amateur only has to ask for advice at the lumberyard. Compare this to using concrete. It takes much more skill, as the people who tried to build a Frank Lloyd Wright Usonian Automatic house found out, and it is even harder if the concrete is to be poured into standard construction-type forms. To build with steel is quite impossible for an amateur.

Among the other money-saving requirements were the use of asphalt shingles for the roofing, aluminum standard-sized window and door frames, painted sheetrock for the interior walls, plywood subflooring (to be covered by carpets or linoleum) for the second story, and only one bathroom. Two more important savings came about as a result of a key architectural decision, to place the bedrooms on the first floor and the living room and kitchen on the second.

MAXIMIZING INTERIOR SPACE

Reversal of the usual layout of two-story homes yielded a number of benefits. The living room could span the entire house without

Placing the bedrooms and the bathroom on the first floor had economic and habitational advantages. Large structural members were not required to carry the upstairs load. The costs of plumbing materials and labor were lower for a downstairs bathroom. Since the bedrooms could be reached directly from the street, they and the living room had more privacy. Although the bedrooms were small (9.5 x 14.4 feet and 9.5 x 11.5 feet), glass doors leading to the backyard made them seem much larger.

the use of large structural members to carry the upstairs load, and location of the bathroom on the first floor would substantially reduce the cost of plumbing materials and labor. The economics were secondary. There were now three privacy zones—the two bedrooms and the living room. It would not be necessary to go through the living room to reach the bedrooms, or to diminish the size of the former by closing it off from view with an entrance hallway.

All three zones could be reached directly from the front door. Acoustical privacy was increased by insulating the bedrooms, bathroom, and floor of the second story. The arrangement also enhanced security. From the upstairs windows occupants could see what was going on outside, and in downstairs bed-

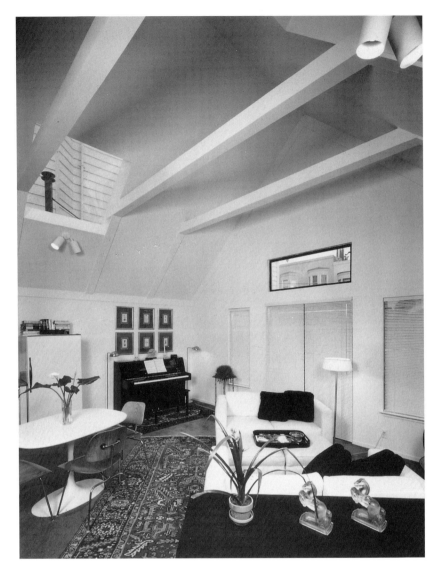

Spanning the entire house, the living room (right) or dining area (facing page) was extended beyond its eight-foot ceiling with a forty-five-degree pitched roof. Large skylights on both sides of the roof, an 8- x 8-foot window in the front, a sliding glass door covered with curtains leading onto a small deck in the back, and clerestory windows on the other walls opened the room to daylight and air. Residents of the cottages reported that the height lifted their spirits when they were in the room.

rooms at night they were more likely to hear an intruder than if they were on the second floor. In addition, someone temporarily confined to a wheelchair or hobbling around on crutches could at least get to a bathroom.

As people who lived in the cottages later reported, the greatest advantage was the airiness of the living room and the light pouring in through the windows. This was achieved partly by an 8- x 8-foot window in the front, a sliding glass door opening onto a small deck that overlooked a private enclosed backyard, and clerestory windows on the sides. But the effect was created primarily by extending the height of the room with a forty-five-degree pitched roof and installation of large skylights on both sides. Filtered floodlights just below the skylights maintained the

effect at night. Because they are switched, the user can turn these floodlights on or off as desired.

Much more than just light and airiness was achieved by the extension of the roof, though. The height, especially with the soaring apex, humanized the space. People in the room perceived the house as much larger and more luxurious than it was. Instead of the oppressive sense of confinement that a box shape with an eight-foot ceiling would have produced, people experienced a lifting of the spirit, a feeling that they controlled the space rather than it controlling them.

Viewed from the outside of the house, the roof evoked the traditional American image of a home. Ask a child to draw a picture of home, and more often than not the pictured house will

The appeal of the pitched roof was demonstrated by its success in conveying the sense of home in a variety of other residential designs, including the mixed-use Two Worlds project in Pleasant Hill, California. (For a discussion of this project type, see Chapter Seven.)

turn out to be a box with a pitched roof, even if the youngster is brought up in a high-rise apartment. The simple form is often used in advertising, and it is the shape of the little token used in the game Monopoly to indicate the purchase of a house. It connotes security, warmth, contentment, rest after a day's work, the return from a journey, release from travail, sanctuary. Many people have commented that as soon as they saw these and similarly designed cottages, they were attracted to them, in some cases without quite knowing why. Over the years, the pitched roof turned out to be a highly successful design element in different types of housing, including multiunit buildings, whatever the scale, massing, or intended occupancy.

Home implies a hearth. Whether the love for a stone fireplace is primordial or merely reminiscent of the "good old days" or of "simpler times," a home needs one. (Indeed, apartment dwellers are often willing to pay a premium if there is a working fireplace in the living room.) Although it was economically unfeasible to build a stone fireplace in the cottage, a fair substitute was provided with a modern metal pot-bellied wood-burning fireplace. For grilling a steak or toasting marshmallows, the fireplace is almost as good as an open stone hearth, and it gives off enough

The conversational layout of the living room centers on the fireplace. The free-standing fireplace allows the room to show its full size.

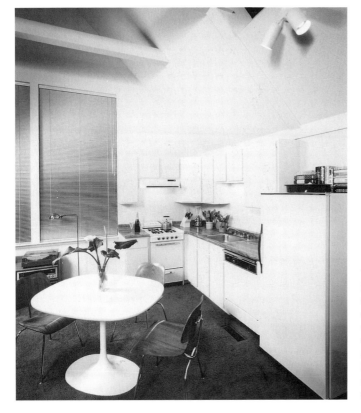

The dining area is conveniently near the kitchen counter. Note the placement of all counters against the walls. This visually enlarged the space and made it multifunctional. This overall second-floor plan has 400 square feet of space. Also, the height of the sloped ceiling, the slope of which begins eight feet off the floor, is an economical way to gain volume and to make a small space look large.

heat to take the chill off the living room on a winter night (or, in San Francisco, on a summer night).

Diagonally across from the fireplace was an open kitchen. The layout effectively created distinct dining and living areas, which flowed into each other so that space was maximized for either function. With the stairs from the first floor snugged out of the way in a corner, the room had more than 400 square feet of floor space available for the usual living room furnishings and a dining table.

On the ground floor, the bedrooms were made to feel much larger than their 9.5- x 14.5-foot dimensions by integrating them with the back garden. Sliding glass doors were used instead of windows, so that when open, the space for strolling and sitting

A loft can be built in the living room above the kitchen for use as a study or storage area, or, if building codes permit, an extra bedroom. A steel strap with two bolts secures the floor of the loft. This vertical structure holds the weight of the loft floor. The weight is carried through to the beam above, which also acts as the top handrail for the platform.

was extended by fifteen feet. Closed, the glass doors created an illusion of space, which was increased by carrying through the design of the interior wall to the eight-foot-high fence (the same height as the bedrooms). The approach to the front door was integrated with the house by means of a small yard and an individual parking space.

Thus the house has two distinct perspectives of space. On the second floor, the perspective is vertical and wide, allowing for an expansive view of the sky and environs. On the ground floor, the perspective is horizontal and narrow. It is cozy, befitting bedrooms, but not suffocating, which would be the case if there were no garden.

When the cottages were sold, the new owners were offered suggestions on how to make the space look still larger. The suggestions included:

- Full-length wall mirrors, starting at the carpet line, particularly in the living room. An armless sofa placed next to the mirror would appear twice as long.
- Mirrors instead of splash boards behind the kitchen and bathroom counters, and full-length mirrors on the inside of bathroom and bedroom doors and outside of closet doors.
- Indirect lighting in the living room, by means of cove lights on top of the kitchen cabinets and one or two floor lamps.
- Two ten-inch-deep shelves around the perimeter of the living room, with the bottom shelf six feet eight inches above the floor, creating a horizontal perspective that would make the ceiling appear considerably higher, especially if indirect cove lights were installed on the top shelf.

Recommendations were also made on how to increase storage space. A lack of places to stow the possessions inevitably accumulated in modern society can be a major problem in large houses, much less cottages. The owners were shown areas where shelves or cabinets could be installed: under the stairs, above doors, over toilet tanks. Not so obvious was the idea of building a loft in the kitchen by attaching it on one side to studs deliberately placed in the wall for the purpose and by suspending the other from the ceiling.

Were it not for code restrictions, the loft could also be used for sleeping (and indeed may very well have been by children whose reading lessons did not include the Uniform Building Code).

THE HOUSE AS AN ARMATURE

Installation of a loft was just one part of a basic design concept, the house as a kind of armature permitting external, as well as internal, expansion. Without much trouble the owner could add on a deck or bay windows or a dormer in the roof. All that was required was the removal of some of the plywood siding, drilling holes in studs, and attaching the additions with bolts. (In some houses built later at other locations, it was possible to knock through the wall between the bathroom and a bedroom to install a door leading to a yard or patio.)

More daring perhaps, but not too difficult, a third story could be built. The pitched roof could be removed, the necessary

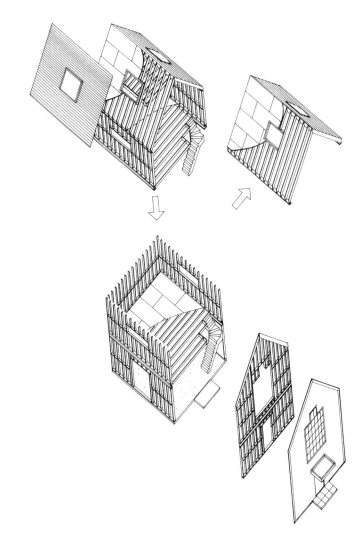

A third story can be added easily by removing the pitched roof, attaching the required structural members, laying plywood flooring, and replacing the roof. Vertical expansion is most suitable for cottages built on small urban lots, where there is insufficient space for horizontal growth. When the cottage is built on a standard one-fourth-acre suburban lot, new rooms, a garage, a carport, or a patio can be added horizontally. To allow for expansion, the cottage should be placed in the center of the lot.

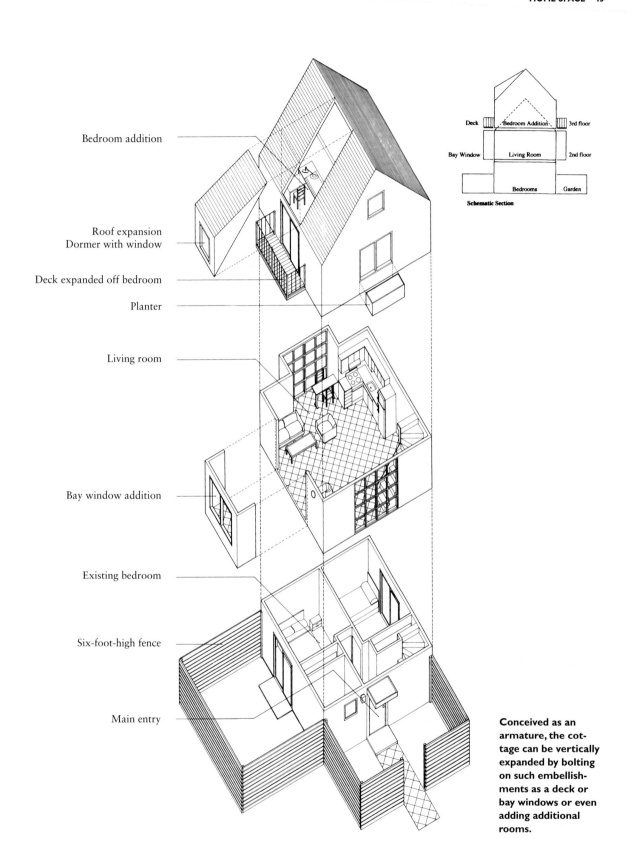

Bedroom addition

Roof expansion
Dormer with window

Deck expanded off bedroom

Planter

Living room

Bay window addition

Existing bedroom

Six-foot-high fence

Main entry

Deck | Bedroom Addition | 3rd floor

Bay Window | Living Room | 2nd floor

Bedrooms | Garden

Schematic Section

Conceived as an armature, the cottage can be vertically expanded by bolting on such embellishments as a deck or bay windows or even adding additional rooms.

structural members attached, the plywood flooring laid, and the roof replaced. Although the owner with modest construction skills could do the job, it would probably be necessary to hire a contractor because of the problems of building vertically. When building horizontally, the owner can occupy the house during construction. Building vertically not only requires the owner to move out and waterproof the structure during construction, but also to hire a contractor to complete the job quickly, as well as a team of assistants to help move materials. Nevertheless, the cost would be relatively low since the house was designed to bear the additional loads and facilitate expansion.

If the cottage were built on a larger lot, though, the work definitely could be done by the owner because the expansion could be horizontal. The lot would have to be the standard quarter of an acre, or at least 4000 square feet, which means it would probably be situated in the suburbs. With future expansion in mind, the original cottage—the armature—should be placed in the middle of the lot. Because the house is square, new rooms and extensions can be efficiently clustered around it in whatever configuration the owner wants.

Thus conceived as an armature, the cottage is a kind of architectural Rubik's cube. The possible variations in design, layout, detailing, and massing with other cottages are almost endless. Plans at each level and between levels can be twisted, shifted, reversed, and changed—indeed the levels themselves could be swung around on their vertical axis.

Interior space can be expanded and contracted. Windows and doors can be placed where they are most convenient, and relocated if need be. The exterior design can be modified to blend in with the character of a neighborhood—or, if an assertive owner wishes, to contrast with the rest of the neighborhood. A few can be fitted into a small lot, or many can be clustered in diverse ways on a large one. The basic cottage concept is enormously flexible.

ENDLESS POSSIBILITIES

Construction of the cottages took about three months, and they were sold within three weeks. Soon afterward more were built nearby, with similar success, and they were followed over the years by many others in San Francisco and across the bay in Oakland. The flexibility of the design concept was demonstrated

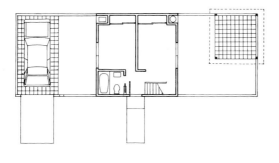

Typical first-level plan. On the left is the fenced-in auto space. In the middle are the two bedrooms and bath, an entry lobby, and a stairway to the second floor. The fenced-in court on the right has a trellised patio area.

Second-level plan showing the kitchen/dining/living area and roof trellis.

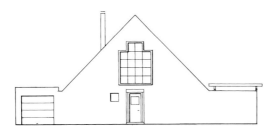

Front elevation facing the street shows the garage door on the left-hand side and the main entry door in the middle.

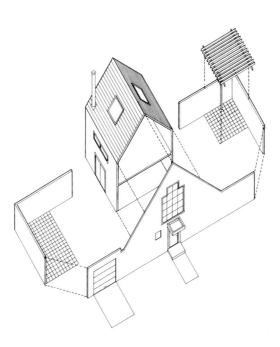

Axonometric drawing showing the street-side facade in its relationship to the 20- x 20-foot cottage and the eight-foot fences that enclose the car park and the trellis patio.

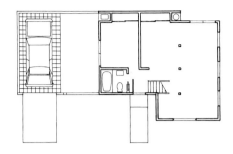

First-level plan showing an enlargement of the bedroom on the right. This could be turned into a work space or an office, leaving the bedroom on the left for private use.

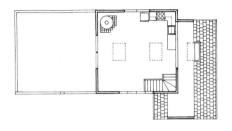

Second-level plan with an unchanged kitchen/dining/living room, but with an addition to the right incorporating a new roof that covers the added space below.

The first-floor room extension of this front elevation mimics the sloped roof shape of the larger house.

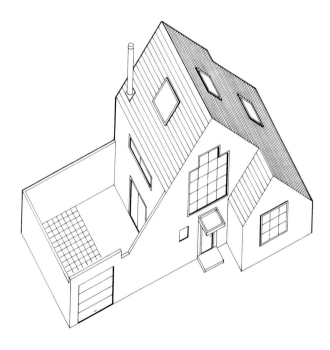

Axonometric drawing of the enlarged first-floor bedroom. The trellised patio and fence, which would have been on the right, have been removed.

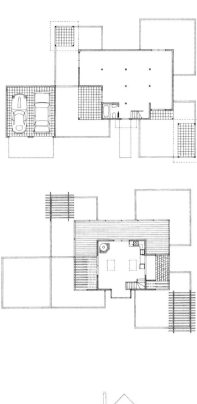

In this layout both first-floor bedrooms have been turned into one
big room. This room can then be
divided into three bedrooms, a
working art studio, or an office
space. It also shows four outside
patios with a trellis, an eight-foot
fence enclosure, and a covered
two-car garage.

Modified second-level plan retains
the original kitchen/dining/living
room floor space, but adds a four-
foot bay extending over the entry
door below. The back part of the
first-floor extension is covered
with a flat roof-deck for use by the
occupant of the second-level living
area. The remaining elements
shown on the illustration are the
extended roof parts.

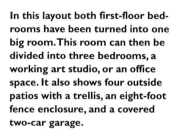

A street-side elevation showing
roof extensions over the first-
floor extended space. To the left is
an addition of a two-car garage.

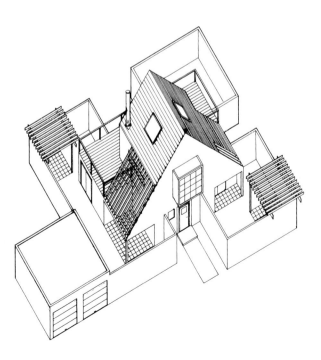

This axonometric drawing of the
fully expanded 20- x 20-foot
armature house illustrates the
many possible spatial additions
that can be accommodated given
this expansion. Livable space
could reasonably be as much as
2000 square feet.

by how well it could be adapted to different sites, the architectural style of neighboring buildings, and market demands.

Like the first cottages, the projects were built on transitional sites. Most were in neighborhoods characterized by old multiunit dwellings, but some were in commercial districts slated for residential development. Because security can be a problem in such areas, the first project was closed off by a high fence with the parking spaces inside. That, and the fact that the houses were perpendicular to the street, created a mewslike effect. For some of the subsequent projects, the feeling of a mews was heightened by grouping the houses around a courtyard. The backs and sides of the houses, along with fences, served as an effective barrier against intruders, and security was increased by the visibility of the courtyard from all the houses.

One project, situated in a somewhat rough neighborhood in Oakland, was laid out like covered wagons around a campfire and encircled by a wall to increase the security. Elsewhere, though, the arrangement was just the opposite—compact, rather like summer cottages at the beach—and in other places the houses were lined up in the usual way on the property line.

In a neighborhood where burglary, robbery, and assault are serious problems, the cottages were arranged in a circle like wagons around a campfire, and the site was enclosed by a wall. As at most of the cottage projects, a parking space was provided in front of each house to enable the residents to keep an eye on their own cars.

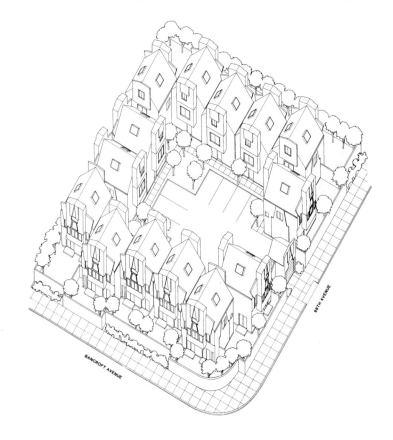

When residents of a neighborhood demanded that the cottages blend in with a Victorian building across the street, Victorian detailing was added to the street-side façades. The modification added ten percent to the cost of each house.

Because of their square shape, the houses could be grouped in a great many ways, depending on the site and best configuration for maximizing ventilation and access to daylight.

Not all the houses were square, however. As an experiment, three of the houses in a ten-unit project were 20 x 24 feet and the internal layout was more conventional: living room, kitchen, and a garage downstairs, two bedrooms and bath upstairs. They were less successful than the 20 x 20 cottages. Clearly, the soaring living room ceiling made a difference.

On the other hand, some cottages at another location were only 12 x 20 feet, but three stories high with a garage on the ground level (which could be easily converted into an extra bedroom or study), the living room, kitchen, and dining area on the second level, and the bedrooms on top. They were quite successful.

At a few sites the endearing external view of the living room—the pitched roof—had to be modified to suit the neighbors' taste. Residents of one neighborhood insisted that the cottages blend in with a Victorian apartment building across the street. A compromise was worked out. Victorian detailing was added to the street-side façades, which increased the cost of each house by $4500 and, as a reviewer pointed out, was less than satisfactory architecturally, although people in the neighborhood were very happy with the result. Another site, occupied by a row of condemned houses dating from early in the century, had to meet the city planning commission demands that the "historic" façades be preserved, characterless though they were. That, like the Victorian façades, increased the cost of the houses. In some cases site-specific modifications, and their added costs, were justified. For example, the exterior façades of a project in a rough section of Oakland (the one laid out like wagons around a campfire) were designed to subliminally suggest a line of husky football players. The idea was to discourage young toughs from entering the compound.

A major problem with modifying the façade is that it makes it harder for the owner to add a story to the house or otherwise change the exterior. The house becomes less democratic. If that results from the cultural orientation of the owners, at least it is their decision. But when political pressure imposes conformity, or planning commissions impose questionable design conditions, it is a serious infringement of an owner's freedom. Compromise is often necessary and very desirable, of course, and so is the preservation of historic buildings or even entire neighborhoods. But the goal should always be to provide a person with the opportunity to create a congenial, individualized home.

On one point there was no compromise: However dense the grouping of the houses, whatever their size, whatever their façades, they were all completely detached, if only by two inches between neighboring walls. The houses and the land they stood on therefore belonged to the owners, without the restrictions or shared burdens of condominium-type ownership. They were private property in the fullest nonexploitive sense of the word, and for better or worse the image of the single-family home on its own land is a deeply rooted American tradition, probably because there has been so much land available in many parts of the country. In many cases separation was a decisive selling point.

HIGH-DENSITY DEVELOPMENT OF AFFORDABLE HOMES

It became increasingly evident in the course of building the projects that cottage construction offered a very practical alternative to multiunit buildings for high-density development. Unit for unit they were at least twenty percent less expensive and were far more desirable. Instead of cells in steel-and-cement blocks, they were homes. They could be built quickly on almost any site and, as investigation of their potential showed, were suitable for a broad range of climates and cultures.

At the request of the government of the former U.S.S.R., a proposal was made to build a pilot project of 500 cottages on ten hectares on the outskirts of Moscow. Cottage construction was seen as a solution to the desperate need for housing in the country and a response to the growing demand during the Gorbachev administration for the private ownership of homes. The government recognized that the traditional high-rise apartment building was inadequate. Since most of the elements were prefabricated, including the concrete skin, completion of a project could be delayed for years when factories failed to meet production schedules—which was usually the case. Because of prefabrication in concrete, designs were inflexible and workers never had the opportunity to learn skills needed for innovative design and faster construction. Moreover, the apartment buildings often began to deteriorate before they were completed, as a result of inferior materials, poor workmanship, and severe weather conditions. Although the proposed design of the cottages was essentially the same as for those built in the United States, except for the inclusion of more insulation, the plan included instruction for people in the construction industry on how to build and maintain the homes. They in turn would teach others. The idea was to develop a resource of skilled construction workers rapidly. It was estimated that 1.5 million homes could be built in a year. Before the plan could be implemented, the old Soviet Union collapsed.

Consequently, the Israeli government requested proposals that would suggest how to house the tens of thousands of people emigrating from the U.S.S.R. to Israel. A similar program was then developed by an Israeli consortium that included engineers, financiers, lawyers, contractors, and the author. Even though timber is scarce in Israel, the structural frames were to be made of wood (imported from North America and precut) so that the immigrants could be taught to help with the construction. To further hasten completion of the houses, parts of the frame would be assembled on benches at the site, then erected, a methodology sometimes used in the United States for mass-produced housing. Once the critical demand for housing was met, the wood-frame aspect of the design would be abandoned in favor of the usual regional construction material, cement blocks. In fact, the design allowed the use of the blocks for repairs of and additions to the wood-frame homes. The style of the house was distinctly Middle Eastern—heavy-stucco exterior and interior finishes, flat roofs, and private patios.

A typical Middle Eastern flavor would also be created by clustering some houses on hillsides in the fashion of the old sections of Jerusalem. The program envisioned construction of about 40,000 two- and three-story units in ten to twelve months, at an

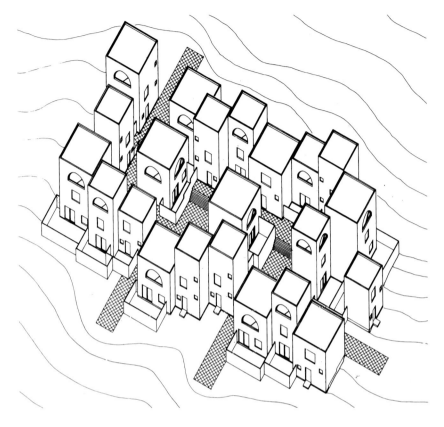

For a proposed project in Israel, the cottage design was modified to fit in with the typical Middle Eastern residential style. Some were to be clustered on hillsides like many homes in the old section of Jerusalem. Heavy stucco, the usual regional construction material, was to be used for the exterior and interior finishes. The houses would also have flat roofs and private patios.

average per-unit cost of about $19,000. Unfortunately, the government—which was sponsoring the project—ultimately decided on imported prefabricated mobile units to be assembled in Canada and the United States and placed on the sites by regular Israeli construction workers. The decision shows their disregard for the site's climatic conditions and traditional building context.

Very different in many respects, but the same in principle, were the efforts by the great Egyptian architect Hassan Fathy to build a new village for the people of Gourna in upper Egypt. The population, whose chief occupation was robbing the ancient tombs on the site, was to be relocated in order to preserve what little remained of Gourna's archaeological treasures. Fathy received the commission to design New Gourna. In his classic description of the project, *Architecture for the Poor*, he explained his approach:

> You must start right from the beginning, letting your new buildings grow from the daily lives of the people who will live in them, shaping the houses to the measure of the people's songs, weaving the pattern of a village as if on the village looms, mindful of the trees and crops that will grow there, respectful to the skyline and humble before the seasons. There must be neither faked tradition

nor faked modernity, but an architecture that will be the visible and permanent expression of the character of the community.[10]

Individual homes were to be built for about 900 families. That did not mean detached houses, though, because it would be contrary to custom born of the need for protection from hostile nature and hostile people. Instead, groups of ten to twenty related families, called *badanas,* were to be clustered around their own courtyards, with each of the larger badanas having its own cafe, grocery, and barber. Fathy explained:

> Now most architects when replanning a village arrange the houses in straight, orderly streets, parallel to one another. This is easy, but dull. In fact, when these parallel streets consist of uniform, minimum-standard houses unrelieved by vegetation or other features, the effect is sordid and depressing. Yet there is no need to arrange houses like this. Exactly the same houses can easily be grouped around a small square. . . . In several important respects the badana is the principal socioeconomic unit of the peasant. I had to take account of this, to make sure that each badana was housed together and given facilities for all the communal activities to which it was accustomed.[11]

Despite the communal orientation, every house would be "a hollow square, turning blind, windowless walls to the outside, with all its rooms looking inwards to a courtyard from which only the sky can be seen. The courtyard becomes the owner's private piece of sky," which for the desert-dwelling Arab is "the kindly aspect of nature, unlike the 'burning, glaring, and barren' surface of the earth."[12] The houses and other buildings were to be constructed of mud brick, and the architectural motifs were to be the traditional vault and dome. Mud brick was chosen primarily because it was inexpensive, but it also had the advantage of being familiar to the peasants, a number of whom received training as masons on the project. Fathy had anticipated that New Gourna would serve as a pilot for solving the acute housing problems in rural Egypt. However, politics intervened. Because the Aswan Dam already limited the amount of silt that could be used for agriculture and construction, the Egyptian government discouraged the use of silt as a building material. Also, many Egyptians would prefer to build concrete block homes, which are there considered a status symbol. In the end, Fathy was removed from the project, and it was not finished.

These projects point out a direction for rapidly and economically relieving the housing shortage in many parts of the world, including the United States. Even though the designs might be quite different, depending on the materials available and the culture, certain basic concepts apply everywhere.

First, the focus should be on houses, because many can be built in much less time and require much less engineering and construction skill than multiunit buildings. Provided that the materials are easy to work with, unskilled labor—perhaps the intended occupants of the homes—can be trained to do the construction. Wood is the most suitable material, and in regions where it is scarce the extra expense of importing enough for the frames, at least initially, as in Israel, is a good investment. In fact, in the proposal for Russia, where there are countless acres of virgin forest, the plan was to import lumber for the first houses in order to give the primitive Russian timber industry time to develop the technology for producing boards in standard sizes and to set up an efficient distribution system.

Second, the houses should be detached unless there is an overriding cultural reason to join them, as in the Egyptian villages. Aside from considerations of private property, which do not apply everywhere, complete separation allows a great deal of flexibility in the grouping of the houses. In Israel, for example, some would have been clustered on hillsides. In Russia they would have been arranged to form small villagelike communities. Detached houses can be formed into tight compounds where security is required, they can be staggered to maximize ventilation and light, or they can be placed between trees, crags, and rivulets. They are adaptable to any site. Fathy could not detach the houses in Egypt, but he followed the principle in the arrangement of the compounds.

Above all, the design aesthetics should express the culture of the community. Instead of houses that reflected Middle Eastern aesthetics, the Israeli government opted for American mobile homes and Los Angeles–type mass-produced boxes. The decision reflected the government's purposeful rejection of the culture of the region, including the culture of the many Jews of Middle Eastern and North African origin. One of the country's leading architects, Zvi Hecker, traced the attitude to the Eastern European pioneers who settled in Palestine before the establishment of Israel:

> Rather than attempting to understand the new land and its landscape, climate, and human culture, the pioneers worked hard to make it conform to the reality familiar to them from the countries of their birth. It was no chance, and from no social need, that lakes were drained and forests planted on barren hillsides. The

greening of the desert as a symbol of Zionism was a faithful reflection of the settler's alienation from, and lack of love for, their new environment.

The struggle for political independence led inevitably to armed combat with the neighboring countries, and turned the alienation of the new settlement into a total repudiation of the cultures of the region. Under the leadership of Eastern European Jews, the Jewish community in Israel created patterns and symbols which were foreign to both the traditions of the past and natural features of the land. The Jews of the East, not yet recovered from their decline, which began at the end of Ottoman rule at the close of World War I, were forced to accept concepts which ran counter to their own traditions. . . .

To my regret, the spiritual sources behind Israeli art are largely remote from the heritage of our region. The symbols and images presented in Israeli art are not grasped by the very society they are meant to express. The rightful place of our culture in the Middle East will be in doubt as long as we ignore the cultures of the other peoples in the region.[13]

The Israeli government's repudiation of Middle Eastern cultural heritage sadly mirrors the attitude toward low-income housing that prevails in the United States. Since the 1950s, the U.S. government has almost overwhelmingly imposed the foreign International style of socialist housing on American ghetto neighborhoods. These projects, with their backs to the street, gang-controlled central greens, and numbingly uniform architecture, have not only failed in their mission to provide occupants with safe, comfortable homes, but have actually further ostracized an already struggling segment of our population. Clearly, it's time for new solutions.

Chapter Three

STUDIO HOMES

All the lonely people
Where do they all come from?
All the lonely people,
Where do they all belong?

John Lennon and Paul McCartney

THE SINGLE LIFE

While the basic cottage mentioned in the preceding chapter responds to the needs of families and couples for low-cost homes, it is unnecessarily large and expensive for a very large group of low-income people who are rarely mentioned in discussions about affordable housing. The group consists of single people: unmarried workers, retired widows and widowers, single parents, young people starting out on their careers, and certain intellectuals who have chosen the lonely and unremunerative contemplative life. Many of them live alone in efficiency apartments, hotel rooms, or lodgings, often paying a large part of their income for rent—as much as seventy percent in some cases. Others are forced to live with their children, parents, or other relatives because of the dearth of low-cost one-room apartments, or must share quarters with one or more other people.

To provide this neglected segment of the population with the opportunity for home ownership, or at least more comfortable living accommodations, a design was developed by the author for a detached "Studio Home" comparable in space and amenities to a one-room apartment, but with the advantages and amenities of

Studio cottage with pitched roof shaped to emphasize the symbol of home. The basic house shape allows for façades to be varied architecturally so they are compatible with the existing community. Shown here is a painted plywood façade. Finishes of board and batten, vertical board with heavy wood trim, and stucco are also available. The sliding glass patio door on this front elevation also serves as the entry door.

a private yard, private entry off the public street, and flexibility for change. The design objective was to build such a house, in compliance with local building codes, as economically as possible so that it could be sold or rented for a monthly payment no higher than the rent of a modest studio apartment in the same locality. At the same time, it had to meet the varied needs of a broad range of single people. What might be adequate for a middle-aged bachelor would not be adequate for a woman with a young child, or for a young person expecting to have a family some day. Since the house would necessarily be quite small, it could also serve as a backyard "in-law apartment," guest cottage, study, or halfway house. It might also be used as temporary housing for a homeless couple or family, which would certainly be less expensive in the long run to build and maintain than placing people in a hotel room subsidized by local governments.

A COMPLETE MODERN HOME

The design process began, as usual, with a study of human functions, particularly as they relate to the appliances and furniture that would have to fit into the one room. One of the main questions was what major household appliances the occupants would need. A refrigerator and a stove were necessary, of course. Many of the people would want an automatic dishwasher sooner or later, so space would have to be made available for one. A stacked clothes washer/dryer should also be figured in because it would be indispensable for a parent with a small child and highly desirable for an elderly person, who might otherwise have to trudge to a laundromat with a bundle of laundry. Since the pot-bellied fireplace was so beloved by people living in the basic cottages, wall space was allotted for a niche to hold a prefabricated wood-burning fireplace.

Basic furniture needs included a sofa bed, a dining table with two chairs, a chest of drawers, and a bookcase or shelves. With space to walk around in, the room measured 196 square feet. In addition, a sixty-two-square-foot loft, to be reached by a sloping ship's ladder, would be built for storage or, in areas where it is legal, for use as a bedroom, computer work area, or den. A pitched roof, like the one in the living room of the basic cottage, would provide ample space overhead for the loft.

That left the closet and the bathroom. A deep closet was created to contain box and clothing storage, and a space that

Sofa bed and a dining table for two behind the sofa. Storage in this living/dining/kitchen area is in the overhead cabinets and above the bathroom and closet. The ladder to the right of the fireplace serves the loft and could also act as a bookcase down below.

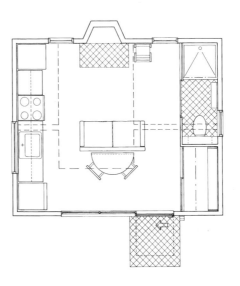

Layout of the studio room at ground level. The washer, dryer, oven and range, sink, dishwasher, and refrigerator are all on one wall to create as much open space as possible. On the opposite side is a bathroom with a toilet and shower stall. The small room on that same wall can also serve as a storage closet or a sleeping area equipped with a bunk bed.

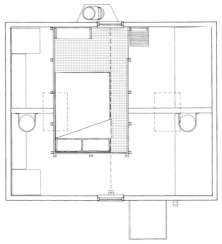

This loft plan illustrates the location of a queen size bed and shows the storage space that is available for use above the bathroom and closet area. The two circles that are shown on the tie beam are small size hot water heaters (two heaters are used for better heating efficiency), one providing hot water for the kitchen, and the other providing hot water for the bathroom.

The loft area with a bed and windows that are operable for ventilation and daylighting.

allowed for construction of a double bunk bed. A toilet and shower were essential. But what about a bathroom sink? Conventional thinking would have it that a bathroom sink is essential, but a spigot could be inserted into the shower pipe for washing and brushing teeth, or the kitchen sink, just a few steps away from the bathroom, could be used. Without a sink, and with a minimum distance of two or three feet between the toilet and shower, a minimum bathroom size of 7 feet x 3 feet would be required. Additional room for the bathroom sink would require at least another 1.5 feet, making the bathroom 8.5 feet x 3 feet, unless one of the expensive small sink types used in campers was installed. Since the bathroom space already measured 3 feet x 7 feet, there would be little room left for a closet. Consideration was given to extending the room a few feet. But that would significantly increase construction costs. They had already been raised more than expected by the necessity of making the front and back walls of the cottage seventeen feet long (fourteen feet for the studio room plus a three-foot depth for the bathroom and the closet). It was decided to omit the sink in the design. If a builder wanted one, a small type could be installed.

Like the bedrooms of the basic cottage, the studio room is extended visually by glass sliding doors leading to a patio or lawn in the front of the house. The illusion of a larger room is also created by mirrored bathroom and closet doors. Skylights in the pitched roof and sliding, clerestory, and small loft-level windows, along with the sliding doors, flood the room with daylight. All but one small accent window can be opened for ventilation.

In developing the design of the studio home, specifications for the appliances, furniture, kitchen and bathroom fixtures, cabinets, doors, windows, and lights were taken from local supplier catalogs. The elements are listed on the following page to give the novice builder an understanding of basic building and component prices.

Since standard and readily available construction materials were specified, the home design can be copied anywhere in the United States at about the same cost, except for land. In fact, someone with rudimentary carpentry skills could build the house with very little difficulty.

EASY CONSTRUCTION

Construction of the wood-frame house was simplified in a number of ways. The foundation, which also serves as the floor, con-

PRINCIPAL CATALOG ITEMS[*]

ITEM	DIMENSIONS (*inches*)	PRICE
Refrigerator	7.4 ft.[3] food compartment, automatic defrost; 2.6 ft.[3] freezer, manual defrost	$400.00
Gas Range	21 x 26 in.	$300.00
Range Hood	30 x 17 1/2 x 6 in. $ 40.00	
Built-In Dishwasher (standard with light wash cycle)	23 7/8 x 25 x 34 in.	$240.00
Combination Washer-Dryer	24 x 27 1/2 x 65 7/8 in.	$620.00
Kitchen Cabinets		
Three wall cabinets	36 x 12 x 30 in.	$240
One wall cabinet	36 x 24 x 18 in.	$ 60
One base cabinet under sink	36 x 34 1/2 in.	$ 85
Two base cabinets with drawers	15 x 34 1/2 in.	$175
Kitchen Sink		
Single basin, stainless steel	25 x 22 in.	$ 40.00
Faucet, single handle		$ 35.00
Countertop, With splash board		$100.00
Heat-Circulating Fireplace (Majestic RC36)	36 in. including fan	$640.00
Sofa Bed	72 x 28 x 26 in. opens to two sleeping surfaces, combinable into one	$170.00
Dining Table	Round drop-leaf, 40 in. diameter	$140.00
Chairs (2), director's style		$ 50.00
Chest of Drawers, six drawers	27 x 15 x 45 in.	$140.00
Water Heaters (2)	20 gal., 22 in. diameter, 22 1/2 in. high	$290.00
Heating System, Thermofilm Radiant Heating System		$300.00
Toilet	18 x 27 1/2 x 28 1/2 in.	$ 60.00
Shower		
Fiberglass base	32 x 32 in.	$100
Plastic walls on three sides	32 x 48 x 32 x 72 in.	$ 85.00
Sliding Interior Doors (2) with mirror panels	69 x 80 in.	$420.00
Sliding Windows (8)		
One double glazed, aluminum frame, left/right	48 x 18 in.	$ 85
Seven double glazed, aluminum frames, up/down	24 x 24 in.	$640.00
Skylights (2)		
Double glazed, operable	48 x 48 in.	$525.00
Patio Door		
Double-glazed glass, three panels, insulated aluminum frame, with screens		$450.00

[*]Prices are approximate (1995), not including lumber, concrete, rough plumbing, rough electrical.

sists of a broad concrete on-grade slab. This technique saves the added cost of a crawl space. The thickened edges of the foundation's perimeter act as foundation beams to support the slab and the concentrated loads of the walls above. The top of the slab surface is then covered with an underpad and carpet. Boards with a cross section no larger than 2 inches x 6 inches are used for the frame, with the exception of the joist for the roof, which is 2 inches x 10 inches. (The 2- x 2-inch joist dimension creates enough dead air space for insulation, but 2- x 6-foot joists would be structurally sound.) Wood structural members are joined with metal joist hangers, corner clips, and tie downs, all of which fortify the wood frame against earthquake and wind damage, and are easy to use.

The loft, supported by a wall and a beam, is made of 1 $\frac{1}{8}$-inch plywood with a board rail surrounding the usable area. Exterior walls in temperate and warm climates consist of 2- x 4-inch wood studs (2- x 6-inch studs in cold climatic zones) sheathed with plywood, which also serve as a structural diaphragm. Fiberglass batt insulation in the walls and the roof is sufficient for almost any climate encountered in the continental United States, and a radiant-heating mat stapled to the bottom of the loft provides enough warmth. (During the winter in cold climates, a portable floor heater might also be needed for the bathroom.)

Doors and windows sold by local manufacturers are usually designed for easy installation by nailing the fin that surrounds the glass window section to the wood-framed wall. Experienced construction workers can build the house in a couple of weeks, while an amateur, working with a helper on weekends, might take about two months.

Altogether, the cost of construction materials, appliances, the fireplace, basic furniture, fixtures, and odds and ends—everything included in the design concept except the land, site development, and utility connections—amounted to less than $15,000 (in 1995). If the dishwasher, washer/dryer, and fireplace had been omitted, more than $1600 would have been saved. In San Francisco, where land values are on the average the highest in the country, the monthly mortgage payment for the self-built home would be about $375, compared with rentals of $500 to $600 for a studio apartment. The mortgage payment was based on the home construction cost of $15,000 and approximate land costs of a typical San Francisco unit basis of $40,000. Because it would be difficult to find a lot for $40,000 in San Francisco, if a lot was

Axonometric viewing the front elevation, showing the cottage construction system and layout of the interior spaces.

Window

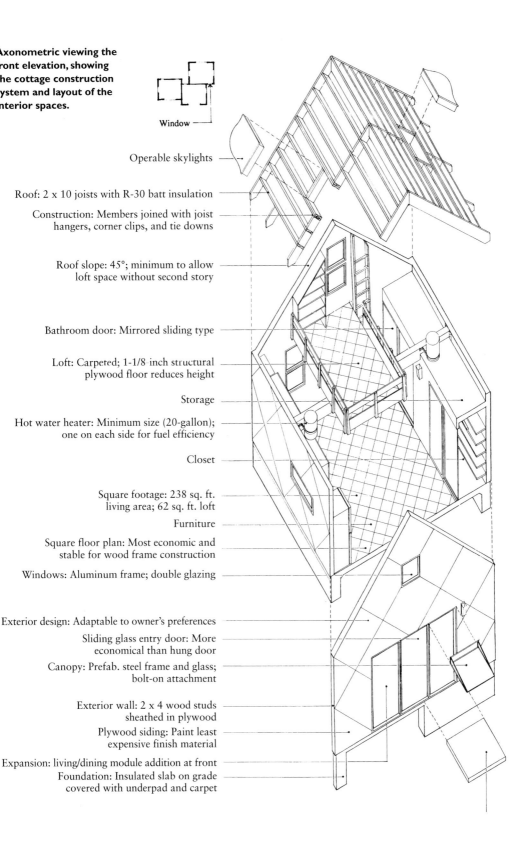

Operable skylights

Roof: 2 x 10 joists with R-30 batt insulation

Construction: Members joined with joist hangers, corner clips, and tie downs

Roof slope: 45°; minimum to allow loft space without second story

Bathroom door: Mirrored sliding type

Loft: Carpeted; 1-1/8 inch structural plywood floor reduces height

Storage

Hot water heater: Minimum size (20-gallon); one on each side for fuel efficiency

Closet

Square footage: 238 sq. ft. living area; 62 sq. ft. loft

Furniture

Square floor plan: Most economic and stable for wood frame construction

Windows: Aluminum frame; double glazing

Exterior design: Adaptable to owner's preferences

Sliding glass entry door: More economical than hung door

Canopy: Prefab. steel frame and glass; bolt-on attachment

Exterior wall: 2 x 4 wood studs sheathed in plywood

Plywood siding: Paint least expensive finish material

Expansion: living/dining module addition at front

Foundation: Insulated slab on grade covered with underpad and carpet

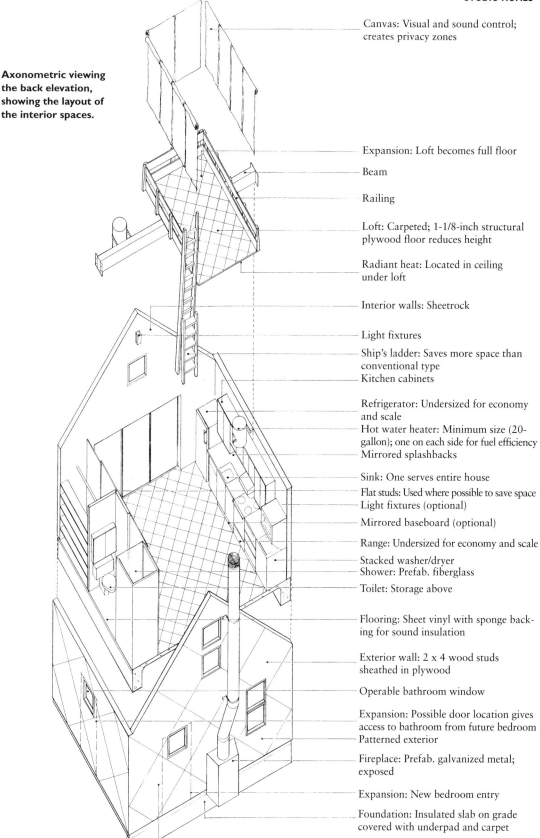

Axonometric viewing the back elevation, showing the layout of the interior spaces.

Canvas: Visual and sound control; creates privacy zones

Expansion: Loft becomes full floor

Beam

Railing

Loft: Carpeted; 1-1/8-inch structural plywood floor reduces height

Radiant heat: Located in ceiling under loft

Interior walls: Sheetrock

Light fixtures

Ship's ladder: Saves more space than conventional type

Kitchen cabinets

Refrigerator: Undersized for economy and scale

Hot water heater: Minimum size (20-gallon); one on each side for fuel efficiency

Mirrored splashbacks

Sink: One serves entire house

Flat studs: Used where possible to save space

Light fixtures (optional)

Mirrored baseboard (optional)

Range: Undersized for economy and scale

Stacked washer/dryer

Shower: Prefab. fiberglass

Toilet: Storage above

Flooring: Sheet vinyl with sponge backing for sound insulation

Exterior wall: 2 x 4 wood studs sheathed in plywood

Operable bathroom window

Expansion: Possible door location gives access to bathroom from future bedroom

Patterned exterior

Fireplace: Prefab. galvanized metal; exposed

Expansion: New bedroom entry

Foundation: Insulated slab on grade covered with underpad and carpet purchased for $120,000, it should be large enough to accommodate three starter houses.

A STARTER HOME

Given some flexibility about down payments and additional fees usually charged by mortgage lenders, almost anyone with a steady income has the wherewithal to buy a house. The lack of such an opportunity has given rise to a vicious circle. As a Harvard study of the housing situation in the United States pointed out, "Young householders find purchasing a first home especially difficult, as housing costs remain high relative to income. Unable to secure a home of their own, these persons remain renters and bid up the price of rental housing." A typical example is the plight of the recent high school or college graduate. Upon getting a job, the first thing the young person wants to do is to move out of the parental home—often to the delight of the parents. He or she moves into a one-room apartment or shares a larger place, in either case paying a larger portion of a meager income for rent. Under the circumstances it is almost impossible to save up enough money to buy a house. Then the person marries and needs an apartment with at least one bedroom. If the couple has two salaries, there might be enough income to build up a savings account. But if a baby comes, the expense of day care, or one parent leaving a job, means there is only one salary again. The baby grows and another bedroom is needed. Perhaps one day the family will be able to afford a house, but probably not for quite a while and possibly never.

The Studio Home can prevent the circle from forming. With a small down payment or on a lease/purchase arrangement, a young person can buy the house and—instead of paying rent, money that is irrevocably lost—build up equity. As with the basic home, the value of the house can be increased by bolting on a planter or two, a bay window, and a canopy over the front door, or by breaking through a wall to install a door and create a patio. Later on, the house can be sold with enough return to buy a larger home, or rooms can be added.

Like the basic cottage, the Studio Home is easily expanded. On a small urban lot, two stories can be built on top of the original structure. On the usual one-fourth-acre suburban lot, the expansion would probably be horizontal, the rooms preferably being added at corners where windows can readily be changed to

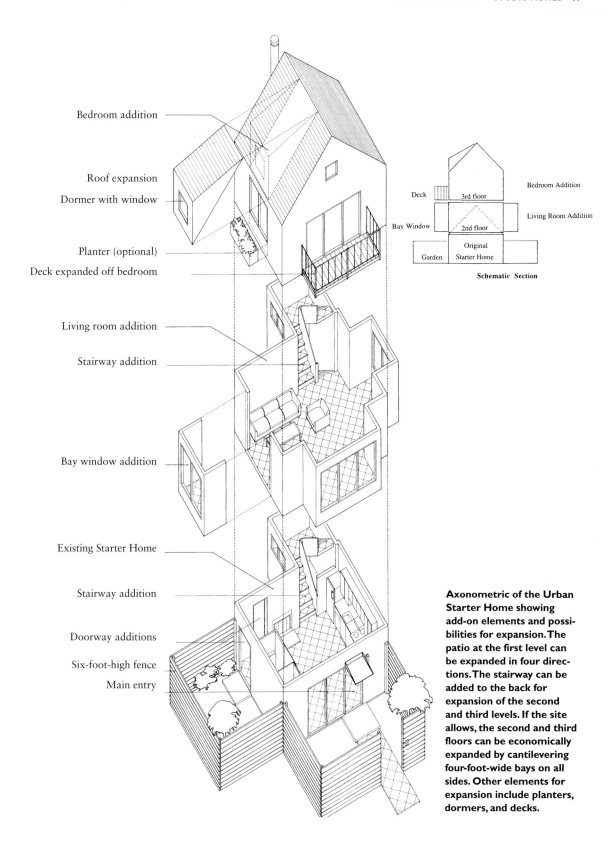

Bedroom addition

Roof expansion

Dormer with window

Planter (optional)

Deck expanded off bedroom

Living room addition

Stairway addition

Bay window addition

Existing Starter Home

Stairway addition

Doorway additions

Six-foot-high fence

Main entry

Deck

Bay Window

Garden

3rd floor

2nd floor

Original
Starter Home

Bedroom Addition

Living Room Addition

Schematic Section

Axonometric of the Urban Starter Home showing add-on elements and possibilities for expansion. The patio at the first level can be expanded in four directions. The stairway can be added to the back for expansion of the second and third levels. If the site allows, the second and third floors can be economically expanded by cantilevering four-foot-wide bays on all sides. Other elements for expansion include planters, dormers, and decks.

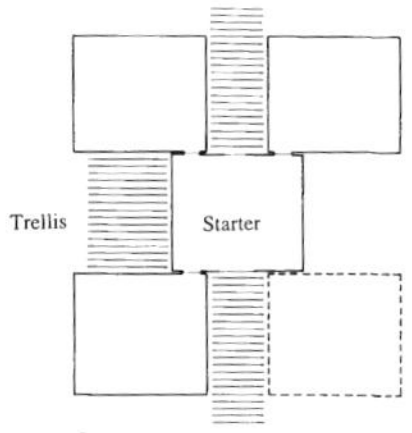

Trellis   Starter

Schematic Plan

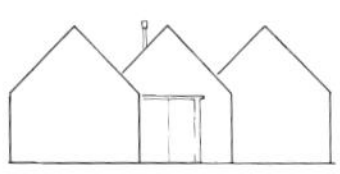

Schematic Elevation

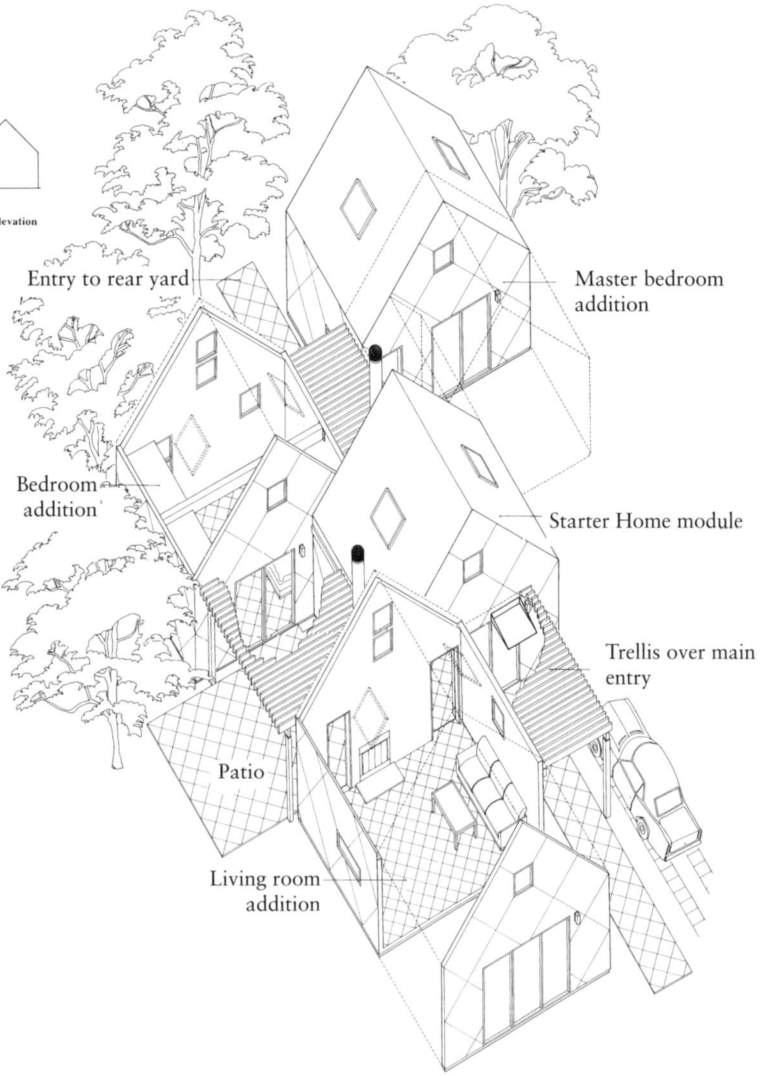

Entry to rear yard

Master bedroom
addition

Bedroom
addition

Starter Home module

Patio

Trellis over main
entry

Living room
addition

Axonometric showing the spatial expansion of the original Starter Home. All four corners of the house allow exterior boxes to be added, which can contain some of the functions that are condensed in the original Starter Home. For instance, one box could be a master bedroom addition with its own bathroom. Another box added to the front could serve as a garage and workshop. A box could also be used to make a new living room, leaving the original house with a kitchen and a comfortable family room for dining and lounging. Off each of these masses are exterior patios, which further enhance the livability of the home.

doors. The cottage could grow into a standard 1500-square-foot suburban house. Whether sold as is or expanded, the studio home can be a starter house—a first rung on the traditional American ladder of home improvement.

AN "IN-LAW" HOME

Because of its small 14- x 17-foot dimensions, the cottage can fit neatly in the one-sixteenth-acre or larger yards behind most suburban and many urban houses in the United States. In most cases, it would cost less than the addition of an upstairs room in the main house and not much more than the renovation of an attic. For a widowed parent forced to live with children for financial or medical reasons, a detached house affords the dignity of independence. People who once have had their own homes cannot help but feel like guests when living with their children, however close the family. Living apart, if only in the backyard, at least creates the illusion of being in one's own home. And for everyone concerned there is much more privacy. The loft should be omitted unless it is needed for storage. If the cottage is for a couple, a 9- x 9-foot bedroom attached to one corner would accommodate a queen-size bed and a chest of drawers.

When a family is reasonably certain that a parent will eventually be moving in, it may be wise to build the cottage well in advance. This offers several advantages. The person for whom the house is ultimately intended would be able to stay in it as a visitor from time to time, making the eventual move less traumatic for all concerned. In the meantime, the cottage could be used as a rental unit, a guest house, a study, or as a transition for an offspring from the cocoon of the family home to the large world outside. Of course, it could also be built specifically for such a purpose.

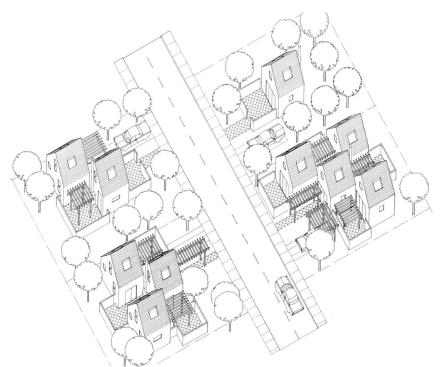

Axonometric showing the different stages, on different lots, of the incremental development of the Starter Home. The illustration shows the house and lot in the first stage of development, then progresses to three modules with expanded patio and trellis elements. This concept of small lots with expandable houses would be applicable in a typical new suburban subdivision.

CREATION OF A COMMUNITY

If one advantage of the backyard in-law cottage is the independence it affords the elderly parent—or a child—the opposite becomes the advantage when a number of the houses are grouped on a site. The lonely single becomes part of a community. On a one-acre urban lot as many as forty units, with a parking space for each, can be clustered attractively in a villagelike setting. With five fewer units or a larger site, a recreation room, pub, or pool could be included.

The community might also be dedicated to single-parent households, in which case there should be a day-care center. This would probably require government assistance. In fact, construction of a complex for indigent single parents would be less costly in the long run than current Aid to Families with Dependent Children programs, and would permit the parents to work. With a lease/purchase arrangement or a subsidized down payment, the parents could build up equity—and the self-esteem they often lack as a result of dependence on a begrudging government.

Similarly, the Studio Homes, built singly and in groups, could be part of a cost-effective, nondegrading program for housing the homeless.

Axonometric showing the Studio Home in an urban setting with vertical flexibility for expansion. This setting shows studio house shapes being used as shops, offices, and single-parent homes. Such a plan is feasible in infill areas where infrastructure is readily available. Project planning for small houses of this type should, where feasible, locate them on and above parking lots so the commute to the areas of employment is eliminated for workers. This unit type can also be placed in a family-oriented community to encourage a mix of families and single-person households.

Chapter Four

HOMES FOR
THE ROOFLESS

If only the government will change its attitude to housing, will remember that a house is the visible symbol of a family's identity, the most important material possession a man can ever have, the enduring witness to his existence, its lack one of the most potent causes of civil discontent and conversely its possession one of the most effective guarantees of social stability.

Hassan Fathy[1]

FROM REFUGEE TO RENTER

After the devastating San Francisco earthquake and fire of 1906, the city's park director, the United States Army, and a relief organization joined forces to build 5610 shacks to house people rendered homeless by the disaster. Ranging in size from 140 to 375 square feet, these "earthquake cottages" or "refugee shacks" were simple one-room wood-frame structures, with wood floors, board-and-batten siding painted green, shingle roofing, and unfinished interiors. They had no plumbing, insulation, or heat, but a wood- and coal-burning stove was provided if the tenant installed a patent chimney. Most were erected at refugee camps established with communal kitchens and toilets in city parks and squares. At one point 16,448 people lived in the cottages.

Tenancy was restricted to people who had never owned homes, and it was decided that the cottages would afford them the opportunity to do so. They were to be sold to the tenants for

"Earthquake cottages" were used to house people left homeless by the earthquake and fire that struck San Francisco in 1906. Assembled by teams of carpenters from prefabricated parts, they were placed in an existing public park. The resultant housing complex was characterized by a tight interrelationship of boardwalks, houses, and streets. Some of these cottages have been remodeled and are in use today.

Typical "earthquake cottage" interior with 1- x 4-inch tongue-and-groove redwood board ceiling. This ceiling was placed below the wood roof rafters to help control heat loss. Note the size of the one-room house, in particular the pragmatic arrangement of the double bed, stove, and wash-up counter on the right.

eventual removal to private lots. The maximum price was sixty dollars, payable in installments of two dollars a month as long as the cottage remained on its temporary site. Payments were placed in a trust account and most of the money was refunded. All but 267 of the cottages were hauled away by the new owners (sometimes piece by piece on their backs) to lots they had purchased or leased or to temporary sites generously made available by some builders. Many became the nuclei of proper homes. A few are still inhabited.

TODAY'S HOMELESS

When San Francisco was confronted with another crisis of homelessness in the early 1980s, the response was very different. Suddenly, the city fathers—like their counterparts in Seattle, Portland, Los Angeles, New York, Washington, and other cities across the country—realized that there were a lot more people sleeping on the streets than there had been just a few years before. Some were "winos," alcoholics who had remained more or less invisible in skid-row parts of town until the fifty-cents-a-night flophouses were torn down as a result of urban redevelopment. Others were drug addicts, many of them aging remnants of the hippie generation, Vietnam veterans brutalized by war, and people originally drawn into their narcotic dream worlds by their yearning to escape, whether from poverty or responsibility, and now hopelessly dependent. Others were the chronic mentally ill who had been denied federal and state Supplemental Security Income due to tightened eligibility requirements and consequently had no money to live on between episodes of hospitalization. Nor did they have any place to go when they were stabilized because of insufficient financing for residential treatment facilities and board-and-care homes. These groups—alcoholics, drug addicts, and the chronic mentally ill—were not unfamiliar. It was only that they were more visible and there seemed to be more of them.

Two groups, however, *were* new to the streets, and the numbers of both were increasing rapidly. One consisted of the working poor who could not afford market-rate housing. Another was comprised of single parents, especially mothers, who were prevented from working because of a lack of day-care facilities for their children and whose income from Aid to Families with Dependent Children did not keep pace with the steady rise in the cost of housing. Both groups were no less victims of disaster than the earthquake refugees, only the disaster was social instead of natural. They were homeless primarily because of the dwindling supply of low-cost housing. As the decade progressed, the disproportion of income to housing costs widened owing to sharp cutbacks by the federal government in government subsidies for residential construction, accompanied by the gentrification of some neighborhoods and the conversion of many formerly subsidized units into market-rate rental and condominium apartments when the government's long-term multiyear agreements with the landlords to maintain low rents ran out. In the early 1990s the two groups were joined by a mounting number of people who had lost their jobs and whose benefits were inadequate or had

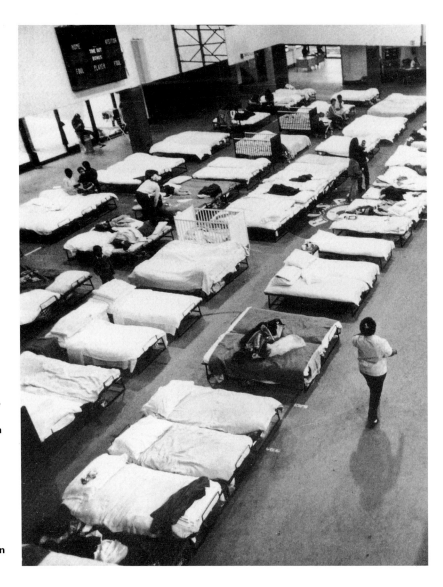

A gymnasium acts as a shelter for homeless families. The lack of wall and ceiling enclosure results in a total lack of visual and acoustical privacy—dehumanizing under any circumstances, but particularly so for families in distress. This is an excellent example of bureaucratic indifference to the privacy needs of families in such situations.

expired. Many were family breadwinners, so whole families were thrown into the street.

Officialdom's response to the crisis, in San Francisco as in other cities, was to provide emergency overnight shelters and dingy rooms in so-called homeless or welfare hotels. The accommodations were as miserable and frightening in San Francisco as they were elsewhere.

A typical shelter is a large room with rows of cots. Long before it opens in the evening, lines of hopefuls form outside because there are not enough beds for everyone who needs one. Admission is granted on a first-come-first-served basis or by lottery. In the men's shelter, guards search them for alcohol, drugs, and weapons, and if any are found, the offender is turned away. Lines again form for the bathrooms. Supper, usually consisting of soup and a sandwich but sometimes a full meal, is served. The night might pass quietly, with nothing more disruptive than the cries of the sorrowful and ravings of the demented, but the guards often have to break up arguments and fights. At 5:00 in the morning the men in the men's shelters are awakened, served coffee and donuts, and then turned out into the streets again, regardless of the weather. Some remain in the streets, preferring them to the regimentation, threatening atmosphere, and indignity of the shelters. Families are turned out at 9:00 in the morning unless they qualify to stay. Family shelters, though understaffed and overcrowded, are open twenty-four hours.

The "homeless hotels" are no better. Inevitably, they are located in one of the worst sections of San Francisco, the Tenderloin, which is infested with drugs, prostitution, and violence. Residents are often afraid to go outside, despite the miserable conditions they have to endure inside. The Junior League of San Francisco reported what it was like for a woman who stayed in one of the hotels with her four children:

> They had all lived in just one small room and there was a bathroom. That was the only good thing about it—it had a bathroom. There was just one double bed. The ants, mice, and roaches shared the place, too. At night she had slept at the foot of the bed, but she never slept well. Meals were usually fast food, or soup cooked on a contraband hot plate. There was no phone, no refrigerator, and no place to do laundry—things most families take for granted. And boy, did the place smell bad!
>
> The landlord had said the halls were off limits. But there was nowhere else to go. Where were the children supposed to play? There was no yard, and it was dangerous to play outside because of the Tenderloin traffic and the weirdos.[2]

An investigation of five of the forty-one homeless hotels revealed even worse conditions. At one, for example, many of the rooms had no windows, no water, and no locks on the doors (some had no doors), but plenty of rats and roaches. No blankets were provided. People qualifying for rooms had to be at the hotel between 5:00 and 6:00, and if they were five minutes late, they were turned away. The 150-room hotel charged the city nine dollars a room per night— that is, a total of $492,750 a year.

The earthquake that struck the San Francisco area in 1989 damaged some of the hotels so severely that they had to be closed at least temporarily. Before the tremblor the city was housing about 1000 homeless a night in the hotels, but took advantage of the closures to cut back the number to about 400 of the most needy, particularly the elderly and the handicapped. Women and families were most often sent to shelters in another county. Some of the slack was taken up by a program that subsidizes reduced rates in hotels for about 1000 homeless who receive General Assistance (GS) from the county or Supplemental Security Income (SSI) from the federal and state governments. Under the program the people paid $100 a week or $270 a month in rent, which in many instances amounted to eighty percent of the person's income. The hotels were of about the same caliber as the one described by the Junior League in which the woman with four children stayed.

That San Francisco's program and others like it did not meet the needs of the homeless became obvious to all but the most insensitive. First, there were never enough shelter beds or hotel rooms. A survey conducted by the municipal government in 1988 revealed that out of 6000 homeless in the city on an average night (6000 was a city estimate; community workers said the actual figure was about 10,000), only about 3000 were able to find accommodations. Most of the rest huddled in doorways, behind bushes in the parks, or anywhere else they could find a modicum of protection from the elements and the marauders who prey on the helpless.

Again, the situation was not unique to San Francisco. The U.S. Bureau of the Census calculated that on the night of March 20-21, 1990, 178,828 people were staying in emergency shelters and 49,783 at selected locations in the street, with New York, Los Angeles, San Francisco, Washington, and Chicago having the greatest number in both categories. That means that out of the total number of homeless, about twenty percent were shelterless on that night. Recent independent studies put the actual number

This homeless man prefers the street to the homeless accommodations that are available in San Francisco. Each night he erects a "campsite," only to disassemble it in the morning and move it with a shopping cart to another site to avoid police harassment.

of homeless at about 2.25 million, and advocacy groups say it is closer to four million. The Census Bureau eventually admitted that its count was far from accurate, terming it a "sample." However, assuming that the twenty percent unsheltered figure approximates the real situation, it can be estimated that from 500,000 to 1,000,000 people spend the night in the street. Undoubtedly, the true figure is higher.

In San Francisco, it was not just the insufficient number of accommodations that was the problem, but the program itself. As a report by the Mayor's Office stated:

> The insidious legacy of the 1980s that had regarded temporary shelter as an adequate response to homelessness must be overcome. Shelters never were and never will be an acceptable alternative to decent, affordable housing. While we must not relax our commitment to offering shelter to anyone who would otherwise be forced to live in the streets, parks, and doorways, we cannot be satisfied even if we have enough shelter beds for everyone who seeks them. Our vision and the overall direction of our policies must remain fixed on the goal of creating and preserving low-cost housing, jobs, and job training programs and the necessary health and social support services that enable people to live with the greatest degree of independence possible.[3]

The report continued to point out the waste of money involved in the shelter program:

> Almost $37 million has been spent by the Department of Social Services since the City's homeless program began in 1982. Had this money been spent in a different manner, it could have financed enough decent, affordable housing for about half the people cur-

rently receiving temporary shelter. In short, millions of dollars are spent on an inadequate system of temporary shelter, swallowing many of the resources that could be used to get to the root of the problem.[4]

Among the solutions offered by the report was the "creation of 6000 new units of housing affordable to people with very low incomes." Included were the "encouragement and support of non-profit housing developers" to acquire and rehabilitate vacant hotels to provide 1500 studio-type apartments (called single-room occupancies, or SROs) at an average per-unit cost of $38,000; construction of 3500 SRO residential hotel rooms and "other types of housing for single adults and youths" ($50,000 per unit); and construction or rehabilitation of 400 "family apartments" ($111,000 each). With other provisions for rehabilitating some public housing units and seismic upgrading and rehabilitation of other buildings, the total cost of the housing program would be about $396 million.

Exactly where the city expected to get that much money was unclear. As the report stated, implementation of the program and other features of the general plan depended "on the availability of resources over which the City has no direct control, most notably federal and state funding for low-cost housing and health and social support services."[5] But during the 1980s the federal government's budget for housing aid declined by seventy-nine percent. The only chance of implementing the program was a dramatic reversal of the government's policy, which was very unlikely. Even if it were to happen, it would be years before any SROs were ready for occupancy because of all the time it takes to acquire property, develop architectural drawings, and complete the construction or rehabilitation of a multiunit building. The program was a pipe dream.

CRISIS HOMES

Good housing is needed now, and there are ways to begin to provide it immediately. One of the ideas behind the design of the studio cottage (indeed, it was the first thought) was to demonstrate that a modern version of the earthquake cottage could be built at much less cost than the SRO and a large number could be ready for occupancy in a matter of weeks. The studio cottages would be suitable for one-fourth to one-third of the homeless population, consisting mostly of the working poor, single parents, and the involuntarily unemployed and their spouses and children. Some two-bedroom cottages or the like might be needed for large families.

The cottages could be built on public property, as they were in 1906. San Francisco has more than 4000 acres of parkland and countless acres of undeveloped site, and the Golden Gate National Recreation Area extending from San Francisco northward comprises more than 73,000 acres. There is plenty of space available for discrete clusters of cottages without interfering with recreational use of the land.

To build, say, 1500 of the studios would require less than thirty acres. A fully furnished cottage would cost about $17,000 plus about $2000 for on-site utility connections—the land would presumably cost nothing—compared with $38,000 per unit for the acquisition and rehabilitation of vacant hotel rooms and $50,000 per unit for the construction of SROs. Four hundred two-bedroom cottages would need ten acres, and they would cost about $60,000 each furnished. While the actual costs might vary somewhat from city to city, the concept is applicable just about anywhere. Many cities suffering from urban blight have underutilized parks or vacant lots that could be used for this specific purpose.

Siting would be of critical importance. Families with children should be placed near supervised playgrounds and buildings where child-care facilities can be established (for example, museums) so that the parents can go to work or seek it. If need be, a child-care center could be built. Single parents should be grouped together as much as possible, not only for the sake of mutual support, including shared baby-sitting, but also to make friends who might want to live one day in a compound of cottages.

The goal should be to sell the cottages to the tenants for removal to their own purchased or leased sites. As with the refugee shacks, a cottage should first serve as emergency housing, then as a permanent home. As soon as a tenant is settled and, in the case of the unemployed, has income, rent should be charged, which could be applied to a thirty-year mortgage if the person elected to buy the house. At 10.5 percent interest the mortgage would be about $150 a month, plus the cost of the land. The city or a knowledgeable voluntary service would help the new homeowners locate inexpensive sites. For example, the added per-unit cost of the land used for a number of cottages clustered on an urban San Francisco site could be about $150. In the suburbs the amount would be higher because of the usual minimum one-fourth acre zoning regulation for a house, however small.

Subsidies and loan guarantees would undoubtedly be needed in many cases. But the basic principle—that everyone has a right to a home, and for people with reliable income, that right should include home ownership—remains applicable.

CITY SLEEPERS

The needs of another, larger group of homeless are quite different and, judging from official housing programs, misunderstood. It consists of the social dropouts, the loners and wanderers, many of them chronic alcoholics, who simply do not fit into the way the world works. At one time these people were the denizens of skid rows and usually managed to find a place to sleep at night, whether a flophouse, mission dormitory, or city shelter.[6] As long as they stayed out of sight, society paid little attention to them, except for the preachers who wanted to save their souls and the charity workers who wanted to rehabilitate them. Now they are very much in evidence, and often choose to sleep outside if the alternative is a shelter or hotel room where they are forbidden to have liquor. Housing programs for these "derelicts," as they used to be called (and are still considered), are inevitably associated with rehabilitative social services.

What most of these people want is simply to be left alone. All they ask for is a secure, dry, and warm place of their own to stay, where they would not be harassed by hoodlums, police, homeowners, and well-meaning authorities who want to change the lifestyle they have chosen. As one alcoholic put it, "There are always places we can go for food, clothes, a shower; what we need is a place to sleep." It is not too much to ask. In a nation as wealthy as the United States, society can well afford to be generous to those who do not fit in and do not want to.

Based on information obtained through interviews with homeless men, a design was developed for a camperlike unit just large enough to accommodate one person comfortably. Dubbed the City Sleeper, it was constructed entirely of plywood, was thoroughly waterproof with caulked and screwed joints, and rested about eighteen inches off the ground on four inverted car jacks that could be individually adjusted for leveling. A door opened vertically so that it could serve as a canopy if the tenant wanted to sit outside. When the door was closed, a sliding window and vents assured adequate ventilation. Because of the Sleeper's snug 8- x 4- x 4-foot dimensions, body heat would create sufficient

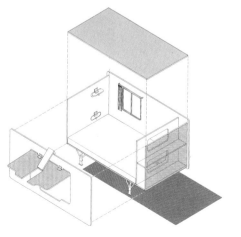

The City Sleeper is composed of six sheets of plywood. The cut-out swing-up door is stabilized with a notched arm so that it can serve as a sunshade or as a roof, protecting the sitting occupant from the rain.

Isometric of the City Sleeper illustrating the way the entry panel works with its latch hooked to the upper ridge piece of plywood. Also note the two shelf storage compartments on one end, and the two high and low vent holes opposite.

warmth at night in San Francisco's mild climate. (In colder climates, slightly thicker walls and insulation would be required.) A four-inch foam mattress provided some insulation as well as a comfortable surface for sleeping. So that the tenant would have a place to store his belongings, such as they may be, a locker and shelf were included. Construction of the Sleeper cost about $500 in materials and $300 in labor.

Two prototypes were placed in a parking lot under a highway overpass, and they were promptly occupied. That was when the trouble began. First, city officials raised objections about the numerous code violations, but restrained themselves from doing anything about it because of the favorable reaction nationwide. Newspaper articles, editorials, TV coverage, a series of cartoons, and countless letters revealed a widespread compassion for the plight of the homeless. According to an editorial in the *San Francisco Chronicle*:

> The temporary little houses are reminiscent of the Earthquake Cottages, produced at low cost and on assembly lines, after the 1906 Earthquake and Fire. These shelters were a response to an emergency as the city prepared for its recovery. The emergency today, it seems to us, is as imperative as the earlier one. And that is why the . . . house merits serious study by all of the agencies which cope with the homeless problem.[7]

While local officials "neither condoned nor hindered" the City Sleepers, as one journal reported, the California Department of Transportation did hinder. Worrying about potential liability if anything happened to one of the tenants, it brought suit to force removal of the Sleepers from its property (it leased out the space under the highway for a parking lot). The department had not worried particularly about liability when the men had slept exposed and unprotected in the lot. Nor had it worried, of course, about the health and safety of the men. The court, expressing reluctance, ordered removal of the Sleepers, and the men went back to curling up in corners of the lot at night.

Had it not been for the triumph of bureaucracy over humanity, hundreds of the Sleepers might have been placed at similar sites and as many more as needed in a variety of locations. The concept was to build them at one or two construction yards, then transport them by truck to areas where the prospective tenants ordinarily spent the night.

That is, the mountains would go to Mohammed, because the permanent homeless tend to congregate in areas where they feel relatively safe and have access to food, bathrooms, and other facilities. However, there would never be more than three at the same spot. Many of the homeless are loners, and can grate on each other's nerves very easily, especially when they have been drinking or using drugs, so the larger the number at one location, the greater the potential for violence. On the other hand, when there are just a few together, they look after each other to some extent.

Obviously, it would not be enough simply to build the Sleepers and dump them somewhere. A coordinated program would be needed, run either by the city or by a volunteer organization with city support. Once a location was selected, consideration would be given to modifying the facades of the Sleepers that would be put there so that they would fit in with the site as inconspicuously as possible. That would be especially important when companies or individuals offered space on their property, which would be quite likely if the program achieved the status of a community project. For the sake of hygiene, chemical toilets of the type used at construction projects should be provided, perhaps not at each site but at a location central to a number of sites. Scheduled cleaning and maintenance would be absolutely necessary. Fumigation would be required often, because experience with the prototypes showed that the tenants changed continually; some men—wanderers by nature—just moved on, others became ill, and some died. The only tenancy requirement should be to keep the area outside the Sleeper clean. Beyond that, there should be no rules, no supervision, and no sermonizing. Let them be. It is regimentation that many are trying to escape, and those who want help will seek it sooner or later.

MINI-GRANNIES AND MADHOUSERS

As a result of the publicity given the Sleepers, a number of other housing designs were created along similar lines, some of them ingenious and eminently practical. One was the Mini-Granny, so named because it was initially intended as an inexpensive backyard in-law unit "for an elderly person as a place to read, be warm, and sleep." But the designers, two pastors of the Holy Terra Church in California, Chuck Ellery and Bill Kaysing, also saw the Mini-Granny as a way to "put [the homeless] under a roof."

Costing about $1200 to build without interior finishing, it was an 8- x 12-foot frame-and-plywood cabin, with a shingle

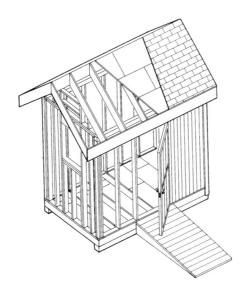

Simple 2- x 4-inch construction that can easily be assembled by one person to create a temporary shelter. These shelters can be built by communities to house the many homeless people who are already occupying the empty lots in their towns and cities.

This Madhouser cabin sits in the shadows of downtown Atlanta.

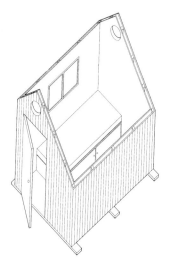

A homeless shelter designed by Pat Robertson is shaped like a house and contains a small space for bed and storage.

roof. The foundation consisted of sturdy 4- x 6-inch skids and 4-x 4-inch crosspieces, into which everything else was locked and braced, so that the unit could be hoisted with a forklift and trucked to an appropriate location. Do-it-yourselfers could purchase the plans and a kit of materials, including lumber cut to size, for about $600. Or they could buy the plans for ten dollars and proceed from there on their own.

More effective in getting a roof over the heads of the homeless were the efforts of a youthful group in Atlanta calling itself the Madhousers, most of whom were recent architectural school graduates. Originally a beer-drinking club, the Madhousers gathered every other weekend in the backyard of one of the member's homes to drink beer but also to build the wall, floor, and roof panels for simple 8- x 8- x 8-foot plywood huts.

They then loaded the panels onto a truck, along with nails, cinder blocks for foundations, and (presumably) beer, and erected the huts on urban sites where homeless men stayed. To the consternation of the authorities, the huts violated just about every applicable code on the books. But as one of the initiators of the Madhousers, Mike Connor, commented, "We're not outlaws. The magnitude of this homeless problem is such that zoning and building codes are irrelevant. The good outweighs any law we might be breaking."[8]

That same compassion, although not the same disregard of the law, was expressed in designs created by students at the Architectural Cluster in Dallas as part of the American Institute of Architects' "Search for Shelter" program. One, for example, was a 4- x 7-foot version of the City Sleeper, designed to look like

The shopping cart concept has the unique feature of being portable. In addition, this design by artist Krysztof Wodiczko, titled *The Homeless Vehicle Project,* expands for sleeping. The cart is a durable unit and can be readily manufactured and distributed to the homeless.

a small house "to give the homeless person the feeling that they have their own little home, their place in the 'American Dream.'" One design conveyed the feeling of a real home by extending the height with a pitched roof.

Countless other ideas have been proposed, all with merit. Taking into consideration the itinerant nature of homeless life, artist Krysztof Wodiczko conceived an elaborate version of the steel shopping cart which could be pushed down the street during the day and converted into a bed at night. E. Gray Beasley, a resident of Washington, D.C., where legislators looking out their windows can see the homeless huddle over subway grates to keep warm, designed a plywood-and-canvas cart convertible into an enclosed bed. Prefabricated storage buildings, garages, and playhouses available from Sears Roebuck & Co. could be used for housing. And the hogans in which Navajos have lived for centuries (and often still do) can be built easily. Nevertheless thousands upon thousands of homeless still sleep in the streets.

PLANNING FOR DISASTER

The bureaucratic indifference to the needs of the people is also demonstrated in the lack of preparation for people driven from their homes by natural disasters. Florida has been struck time and time again by hurricanes, yet after hurricane Andrew destroyed thousands of homes in the state, it was days before shelter was provided for the victims—and shelter consisted only of army tents pitched on muddy, mosquito-infested land. As one person observed, such encampments might be all right for marines, but not for ordinary citizens, especially children and the elderly. Hurricanes along the Atlantic and Gulf coasts, tornadoes in the Midwest, earthquakes in California, typhoons and volcanic eruptions in Hawaii, and fires, floods, and blizzards wreak destruction year after year, and officialdom still depends on ad hoc arrangements in schools and armories for emergency housing.

To show once again that there are inexpensive solutions to the problems caused by such destruction, I developed a design for a mobile housing unit that could be rapidly dispatched by the government to the scene of a disaster. Absent more appropriate accommodations, the unit could be used as emergency housing for the homeless. It might also be purchased or built by a family for use as a camper.

The principal element of the unit is a 4- x 4- x 8-foot box that can be easily assembled using marine-quality plywood panels, lumber of various sizes for the frame and interior parts, a Plexiglas window, and miscellaneous hardware. All the materials can be purchased for about $500 at stores that sell building supplies. When not in use as emergency housing, the box serves as a storage container for the equipment that a family of four would need to survive independently for about a week. Included is a complete utilities system consisting of a two-burner propane stove, a propane heater, a refillable cylinder of propane gas, and a portable toilet, along with other standard camping equipment such as gas lamps (two), sleeping bags (four), 72- x 48-inch foam mattresses (two), a two-gallon steel-belted water jug, a forty-quart steel-belted cooler, a set of cookware and utensils, four

The rectangular panel in this camper is secured with wing nuts so that it can be easily removed. Once removed, the panel becomes a tabletop. The lower panel on the left contains a slide-out counter with a sink, and the one on the right contains a tent and support poles for the camper enclosure.

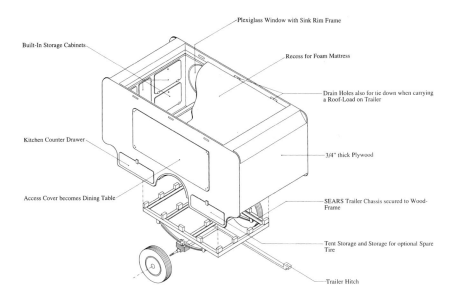

Built-In Storage Cabinets

Plexiglass Window with Sink Rim Frame

Recess for Foam Mattress

Drain Holes also for tie down when carrying a Roof-Load on Trailer

Kitchen Counter Drawer

3/4" thick Plywood

Access Cover becomes Dining Table

SEARS Trailer Chassis secured to Wood-Frame

Tent Storage and Storage for optional Spare Tire

Trailer Hitch

The camper's plywood box structure sits on a ready-made trailer chassis.

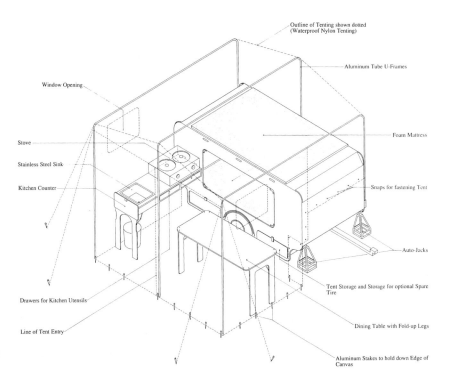

Outline of Tenting shown dotted (Waterproof Nylon Tenting)

Aluminum Tube U-Frames

Window Opening

Foam Mattress

Stove

Stainless Steel Sink

Kitchen Counter

Snaps for fastening Tent

Auto-Jacks

Tent Storage and Storage for optional Spare Tire

Drawers for Kitchen Utensils

Dining Table with Fold-up Legs

Line of Tent Entry

Aluminum Stakes to hold down Edge of Canvas

Detail of the camper when it is fully expanded.

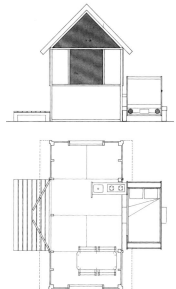

Elevation and floor plan show the further expansion of a small house by using the camper as a starter unit. It has no electricity or plumbing, can be placed on any terrain, and can be easily constructed by even the most unskilled carpenter.

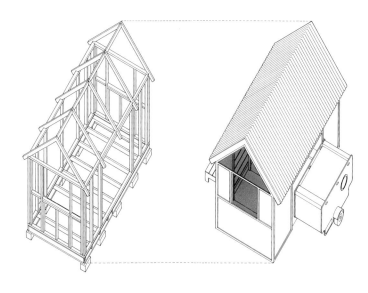

Structural skeleton showing the method of supports for the floor, walls, and roof of the camper-expanded house. The completed camper unit has a corrugated metal roof.

director's chairs, and a radio—perhaps a two-way. All are available from Coleman and Sears. (A family would be well advised to store some clothes, canned food, and a five-gallon bottle of water in the box, making sure to replace the water once a month.)

An 8- x 12-foot nylon tent is stored in a bin under the floor. The box rests on a 56- x 44-inch trailer chassis, ready to be hooked onto a car at a moment's notice.

When needed for housing, the box is transformed into the core of a spacious camper. Fastened to the outside of the box and supported by folding legs is a kitchen counter with drawers for flatware and utensils and space for the stove. (It is stored in a compartment underneath the box.) The rectangular access panel to the box has hinged, fold-down legs so that it can be pulled out for use as a table. Cabinets are built into the two four-foot walls. Two people can sleep on the floor, and two more on the roof; there is ample room for a mattress and two sleeping bags on both floor and roof. The tent is set up in three U-frame extension poles that slip into brackets to form a canopy during the day and can be closed at night for protection against the elements.

In the event that long-term housing is needed, the tent could be replaced easily and inexpensively with an 8- x 16-foot one-

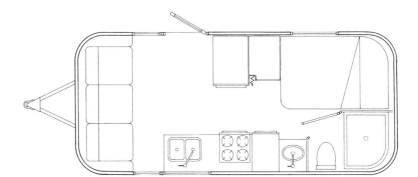

Typical small trailer layout with a double bed, bathroom, kitchen, and lounge area.

room house much like the earthquake cottage, although more commodious because of the equipment and amenities provided with the box. Essentially a larger version of the box, the house is constructed of fourteen 4- x 8- x ³/₄-inch plywood panels, forty 2- x 4- x 8-foot boards for the walls and roof joists, Plexiglas for the windows, and miscellaneous hardware, with a floor and deck made of 2- x 6- x 8-foot boards covered with plywood, two wood-panel doors, and fifty-six 1- x 2- x 8-foot pieces of wood trim. The foundation consists of concrete blocks, and the roof is corrugated metal. Again, the materials can be bought at a building-supplies store. The cost in 1995: about $2500.

Thousands of the boxes, on their chassis, could be stored at depots strategically located throughout the country. Army and air transport would be used to take the units to the site of a disaster. Besides serving as foundations, the chassis make it possible to load the boxes quickly and transport them from landing fields or depots to parks or other land designated as emergency camps. As soon as conditions permitted, individuals would pick the units up at the camp, with their own or neighbors' cars, and take them to their own property. Water and rations could be placed in the boxes at the depot before loading them on transports, or could be provided at the camps. When the emergency was over and permanent housing available, the boxes would be returned to the depots.

There is a more elegant solution to emergency housing problems than the box, but it would be more expensive: the Airstream trailer, or something like it. Those marvelously compact homes on wheels have everything required for comfortable living, from real beds and full stoves to showers and private toilets. But since officialdom begrudges the homeless the least housing, it is, unhappily, beyond hope that it would provide the best.

Chapter Five

CREATING
THE URBAN VILLAGE

I have come to recognize only one supreme art, the art of becoming human, the art of expressing and intensifying one's conscious humanity by appropriate acts, fantasies, thoughts, and works. . . . This, then, is the task for today and tomorrow: to restore and eventually to elevate even higher than ever before the organic and human components that are now missing in our convulsively dynamic and over-mechanized culture. The time has come for architecture to come back to earth and to make a new home for man.

Lewis Mumford[1]

ARCHITECTURAL NEGLECT

Mumford's words bring to mind the social concern that Alvar Alto, Frank Lloyd Wright, and other prestigious architects of more than twenty years ago expressed. This concern is not found in today's well-known architects. Michael Graves, Peter Eisenman, Richard Meier, and Frank Gehry have contributed nothing to the social fabric of the country. Eisenman and Graves, in particular, have developed an architectural vocabulary that is not understood by most people and barely by those that teach it in our architectural schools. Their building images are forced upon student architects as the avant garde of the moment, one that is completely out of touch with the needs of our people.

Alvar Alto, the famous Finnish architect of the 1940s and 1950s, designed housing for the common man. His social concerns were integrated with his total professional philosophy and built works. Alto's housing complexes in Helsinki, Finland, were probably the most interesting manifestation of his social concerns. These projects are in use today and remain as viable to the user as when they were conceived. Many architects today do not accept these commissions as they feel the construction budgets are too low to do exciting architecture, and the architectural fees are not substantial.

Frank Lloyd Wright developed the Usonian Automatic House (see Chapter One), a concept that empowered the layman to build his own home. The Automatic House design revolved around a custom-made block form made from sheet metal that could be fabricated by a local sheet metal shop. From this form a concrete block could be molded and then placed in a wall, roof, or floor position. The thought of creating a form that most people could use to fulfill their housing needs without the help of union craftsmen is a fine example of Frank Lloyd Wright's belief that America had the obligation of adequately housing all its inhabitants—if not through self-built units then through other, more traditional housing.

Graves and Eisenman have not addressed society's basic needs, nor have they contributed to the movement responsible for designing and building affordable residential housing projects. Over the last five years I have commented, in public lectures, on the failure of our leading architects to become involved in plans for this building type. Only now, in mid-decade, do I see a debate developing over whether architecture should be dealt with as pure art—as it is treated today by most elite architects—or whether it should accommodate social responsibility. In the past this was not a debatable point, nor should it be so today. Architecture should be a form that integrates purely artistic concerns with social issues, one that involves the user in the design process, from conception on. Strong architectural designers can deal with public participation. Only those architects who insist on staying in their ivory towers will be adversely affected when the public becomes actively involved in the design process.

The team of Charles Moore, a nationally known people's architect who died in 1994, and Jimmy Burns, a writer and group problem-solving facilitator, developed an innovative technique, called "take part," that ensured effective public participation in the architectural process. They held "discovery sessions" in which the public participated in the creative aspects of design by taking part in charrettes held in community halls during the initial start up time, when the building project was being conceived. The

Charrettes

intent was to make sure that valuable input from community residents was not overlooked and that people's input concerning their own neighborhoods was included in the design concept. Many political concerns in a new project can be resolved at this initial point of the process as well. At the very least, the potential opposition will understand the truth about what is intended for the new site. Many public protests against new construction are based on untruths and lies, and "taking part" is a way to clear the air and alleviate problems before they get out of hand.

Some development firms are attentive to the needs of the people they serve. One example is MacDonald Architect's client for the Frank G. Mar project (described below), the East Bay Asian Local Development Corporation (EBALDC). Their leadership is dedicated to listening to the users' needs, from health to education to living accommodations. When our firm joined forces with them on the Mar project, we brought together two groups of like minds. Consulting the prospective users (tenants), allowing them in on the reviews of the initial planning process, and listening to their concerns helped us as designers to create a very economic and useful floor plan, site plan, and exterior facades.

Jane Jacobs once told about the experience of a social worker who had frequently visited a New York housing project and "was astonished by how often the subject of the lawn came up, usually gratuitously as far as she could see, and how much the tenants despised it and urged that it be done away with. When she asked why, the usual answer was 'What good is it?' or 'Who wants it?' Finally one day a tenant more articulate than the others made this pronouncement: 'Nobody cared what we wanted when they built this. They threw our homes down and pushed us here and pushed our friends somewhere else. We don't have a place around here to get a cup of coffee or a newspaper even, or borrow fifty cents. Nobody cared what we need.'"[2]

THE POOR, THE ELDERLY, AND THE IMMIGRANTS

Both protests articulated by the unhappy New York project dwellers—the failure to consult prospective tenants and the distance from stores—were very much in mind when plans were developed for the Frank G. Mar low-income housing project in Oakland, California.[3] Named for a deceased minister who had worked tirelessly with nonprofit organizations and public officials to raise the necessary funds, the project was to be built in the city's downtown Chinese neighborhood. During the late 1970s and 1980s Asian immigrants, primarily refugees from Vietnam, Cambodia, Laos, Thailand, and China, had crowded into the neighborhood. It rivaled San Francisco's Chinatown for the density of its population and as a regional Asian shopping center. A large percentage of the residents were poor, many barely earning the minimum wage, and much of the housing was substandard. Residents of the surrounding area, which would also be served by the project, were mostly low-income African-Americans.

The project had a dual purpose. The primary goal was to provide "quality and affordable housing for the poor, the elderly, and the immigrants," as Reverend Mar's wife explained. Secondarily, it would contribute to the redevelopment of downtown Oakland.

A unique combination of requirements governed the design. The project was to respond to the desperate housing needs of families, including large ones, who were especially hard put to find affordable homes. But it was also to include units for the elderly and a child-care center, with an outside playground. For the sake of the tenants and as part of the redevelopment of the area, the project was to include stores and other commercial space facing the street. And there would have to be on-site parking. All this was to be done on three-fourths of a city block with a construction budget of only $12 million.

Out of the apparent chaos emerged a diversified community containing different types of housing, along with a variety of stores and a multilevel garage. Residential and commercial usages were kept from impinging upon one another by confining the stores to the ground level and building the housing around a courtyard on the second level, which was reached directly from the street. Originally, the plan was to have only enough parking spaces for the tenants, located on the same level as the stores, but the city paid for two underground levels of structure for use as a municipally owned public garage.

At the urging of community leaders, particularly Reverend Mar before he died, special consideration was given to the needs of the elderly. Through their spokesmen the seniors made it known that they would definitely prefer to be housed in a centered corridor apartment building for security and social reasons, but most of all they wanted the entrance from the street to be locked. (For added safety, the manager's office was placed near

Aerial photograph of the Frank G. Mar Housing/ Commercial Complex, surrounded by parking lots and a mixture of one-, two-, four-, and seven-story buildings. This is the neighborhood's only project with pitched roofs, a detail that to many is symbolic of home.

A building section that passes through the family units on the left and the seniors' residential tower on the right. Below the residential tower is a commercial space that borders on the street-level parking spaces. The permanent residential parking is at the bottom level. The top two levels of parking, owned by the City of Oakland, are rented to the public.

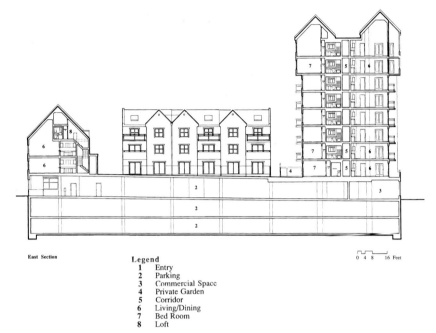

East Section

Legend
1 Entry
2 Parking
3 Commercial Space
4 Private Garden
5 Corridor
6 Living/Dining
7 Bed Room
8 Loft

0 4 8   16 Feet

Second-level plan where the housing units are set in place. The pedestrian streets are the narrow passageways that run parallel with the outside building perimeter. Fenced yards act as transition zones, offering privacy from the social activity of the central court.

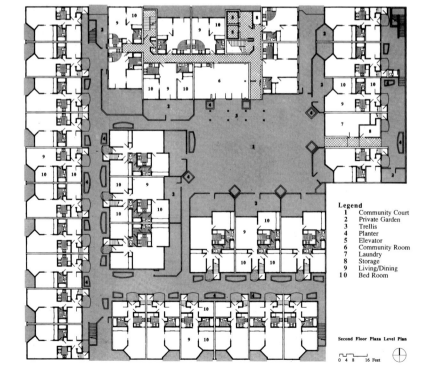

Legend
1   Community Court
2   Private Garden
3   Trellis
4   Planter
5   Elevator
6   Community Room
7   Laundry
8   Storage
9   Living/Dining
10 Bed Room

Second Floor Plaza Level Plan

0 4 8   16 Feet

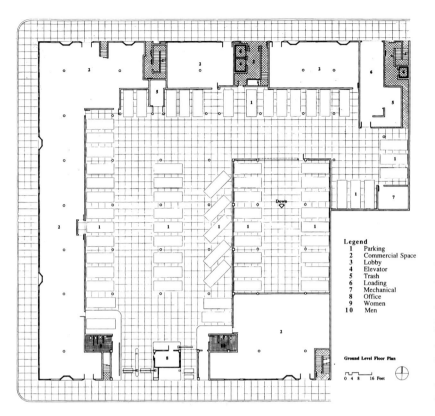

Legend
1   Parking
2   Commercial Space
3   Lobby
4   Elevator
5   Trash
6   Loading
7   Mechanical
8   Office
9   Women
10   Men

Ground Level Floor Plan

0 4 8   16 Feet

Street-level floor plan with a day-care center in the lower right-hand corner and commercial shops along the street facades. The size of the entry to the complex was kept small. The money saved by not having a big lobby area was used in the interiors of the residential units.

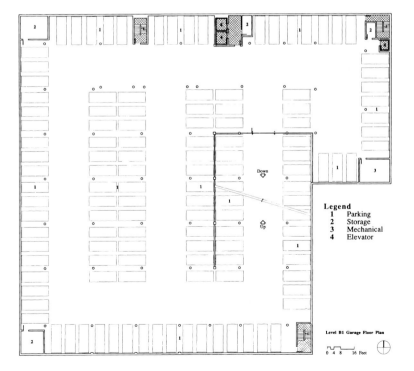

Legend
1   Parking
2   Storage
3   Mechanical
4   Elevator

Level B1 Garage Floor Plan

0 4 8   16 Feet

Typical lower parking level layout. The ramp on the right connects all three levels of parking.

One line shows the number of rooms per unit existing in the neighborhood where the project was to be built. The second line shows the rooms per unit throughout Oakland. The graph indicates that the neighborhood's high percentage of low-room-number units is out of proportion to the overall Oakland profile. One of the goals of the Mar project was to bring some balance to the community composition by creating a proportional mix of larger units for families.

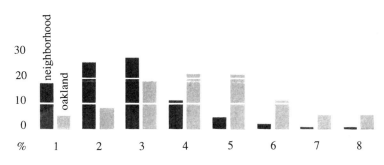

rooms per unit

The number of persons per unit in the neighborhood compared with Oakland. Note that the category for single-person households is very high compared with the city average. This indicated the need to build family units to create a balanced community and to put the project neighborhood household composition on a par with the rest of Oakland.

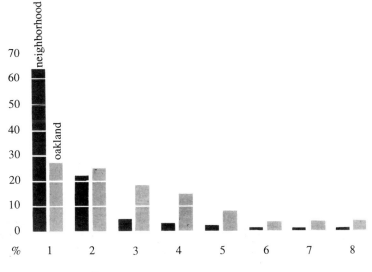

persons per unit

Asian households have more people living in one room than Oakland's other households have.

The ideal unit size (number of bedrooms) and mix of unit types for the new project. This mix meets the neighborhood's need for larger units, and brings the overall neighborhood mix in line with the overall city pattern for multifamily units.

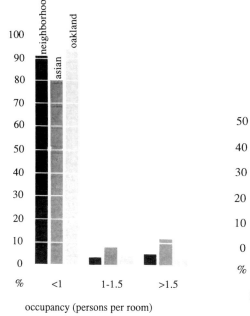

occupancy (persons per room)

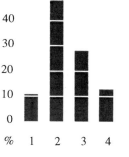

ideal unit size (bedrooms)

the entrance with a view of the door and elevators.) Despite budgetary problems, it was decided to build a nine-story tower containing fifty-one one-bedroom apartments exclusively for the elderly, and also fifteen two-bedroom units for small families. The latter were badly needed, and it was felt that one child on a floor would not be excessively disturbing. Apartments in front of the building looked out on the stately U-shaped Oakland senior-care facility, with a large lawn between the wings, across the street. Those in the back looked out on the courtyard and had a view of the skyline over the low-rise buildings in the rest of the project. Thus, although the apartments were compact, all of them had a spacious and bright feeling.

The expense of building the tower consumed about one-half of the residential budget, and the question was how to build as many units as possible for families with the other half and how many bedrooms per unit were required. To develop guidelines using the latest U.S. census report, a study was made of the occupancy patterns of housing in the area served by the project, particularly how many rooms per unit in our neighborhood compared with all of Oakland. A comparison of the number of people per room in the area, in the city, and among Asians indicated an inadequate supply of family-size units in the area and a relatively high need by Asians for large units to accommodate large extended families. Asians were singled out because they comprised more than half the population of the area and were a much higher percentage of the families eligible for government rent subsidies.[4] In addition, some had first choice on units because they had been occupants of housing demolished during the 1960s in urban-renewal (dubbed "urban removal" by displaced residents) programs that had destroyed the original Oakland Chinatown centered in the area. The land acquisition for the project was a grant from the city.

The Mar project was a long-awaited restitution for past abusive practices on the part of the Le Corbusier–type thinkers who controlled housing and redevelopment agency boards. On the basis of the results of the study, along with architectural and financial considerations, an ideal mix of unit sizes matching that of Oakland's existing needs was formulated for use as a planning model.

The mix actually built conformed closely to the model, except that one-bedroom units were included only in the tower: twenty units with two bedrooms (plus the fifteen in the tower), twenty-seven with three bedrooms, and six with four bedrooms.

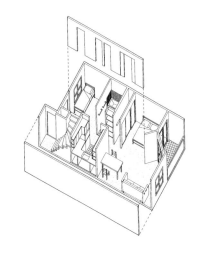

Axonometric of interior
layout of two-bedroom flat.
The double entry door to
the bedroom accommo-
dates an overflow of guests
from the living room area.

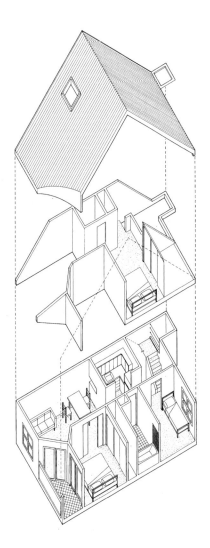

Axonometric of two-story
three-bedroom town-
house. The high ceiling
space above the master
bedroom and the living
room could be platformed
in the future to expand
the floor area.

COMMUNITY PARTICIPATION

As often happens, necessity bred innovation. During the early planning stages of the project, the intention had been to construct a more or less traditional low-rise building. But the tower changed that. Economics limited the number of family-size units, and the space available atop the stores lent itself admirably to a townhouse–type solution. A preliminary design was developed for five three-story wood-framed buildings grouped around the courtyard. Every building was divided into what looked like detached houses, each with its own pitched roof to emphasize the image of home.

Adhering to one of the principles articulated in Oscar Newman's book *Defensible Space*—that each home should have a private entry separated from the publicly used walkway—we created a small concrete platform at each entry door of the housing units on the plaza level.

On the first floor of most of the modules is a two-bedroom flat. The residential module is composed of a flat and a townhouse. The townhouse is on top of the flat, and the side walls are in alignment to economically transfer the vertical loading created by these structures. The bathroom and kitchen plumbing are also vertically aligned one upon the other. This structural alignment is used in mass residential buildings to help bring the construction costs in line, thus creating affordable housing. The second and third floors are devoted to three-bedroom units and four-bedroom units designed like townhouses, with a skylit cathedral ceiling rising more than two stories to the pitched roof over the living-dining area.

The flats and townhouse units have their own plaza-level entrances. Six of the modules are four-bedroom townhouses. The four-bedroom unit is composed of two floors; the first floor, at the second level above the plaza, contains three bedrooms and a living-dining area. The second floor of this elevated unit contains a looming cathedral ceiling over the fourth bedroom. Every unit has a deck, in the form of either a backyard for the first-floor flats or a second- and third-floor balcony for the others.

The next step in the design process, the review of the layout of the units by groups of prospective tenants, was taken with a great deal of trepidation because the users' groups were from such varied social and cultural backgrounds. There were families from Vietnamese refugee camps, from the slums of Oakland and others; there were elderly single men who could not speak

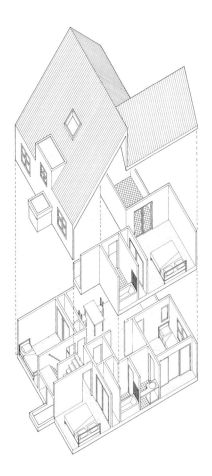

Axonometric of four-bedroom townhouse shows that the lower bathroom is split into three compartments. It is accessible from two sides to accommodate a large family with heavy traffic in the washing and bathing area.

English. A number of different Asian cultures were represented, as well as African-Americans and Caucasians, and the potential for not satisfying everyone—or dissatisfying everyone—was high. An able EBALDC staff sensitized the architectural team to the cultural and social issues involved, and through constant verbal interchanges with all participants, and listening to all the voices, we worked toward the best resolution possible.

To facilitate the review, $1/2$":1' models of the three preliminary designs were built. Our staff developed a three-dimensional model system that was large in scale so the layman could better visualize the real space. The model was composed of lightweight cardboard with movable walls. This allowed viewers who could not read two-dimensional drawings to get a better understanding of the interior space of the unit. Not only that, the model could be cut and pasted to accommodate changes in the layout in a minimum amount of time and at minimum expense.

The groups were advised that any changes they wanted would be made if at all possible. The only immutable restriction was the square footage of the units, which had to be maintained in order to control future construction costs.

Only a few changes were requested, and they were relatively minor. The most important concerned the kitchen. Some people complained that it was too small, so we enlarged the kitchen and opened it to the living-dining room. But when the new layout was submitted to the groups for approval, it was criticized by several Chinese, who pointed out that the traditional stir-fry method of cooking in woks often created a lot of smoke. They preferred a closed-off kitchen. The design was revised accordingly and we closed off the kitchen but left a pass-through area for serving to the living room.

Another criticism was that there was no place in the bathroom to hang the laundry. Asians, it was explained, often wash their clothes by hand. One suggestion was to provide more space for a clothesline by removing the shower door, but that would not be acceptable to non-Asians.

The solution chosen was to build higher fences that extended around the back ground-floor yards and to cover the vertical part of the upper level-deck railings and tower balconies with opaque glass, so that washing could be hung outside but out

View from central courtyard of various decks and opaque glass railings that provide privacy and obscure hanging laundry.

Clockwise: Axonometric of ceiling space above the bedrooms and living room that has been created for an internal expansion of the townhouse unit; an expansion of a two-bedroom unit through construction of double-sized bed platforms; an extension of the second level being used as an additional conventional bedroom.

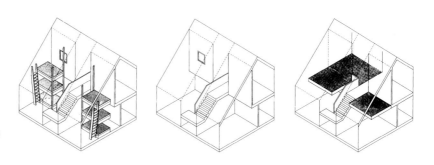

of view of passersby. A slightly smaller tub was specified for the bathroom to provide more space in the room for washing.

One other complaint was easily resolved. Asians asked that the door between the bedroom and living-dining room be enlarged so that the bedroom could be used for entertaining when relatives and friends visited. Double doors were therefore specified.

Surprisingly, no one objected to the compactness of the family units—the floor space is only 600 square feet for the two bedrooms, 920 square feet for the three bedrooms, and 1120 square feet for the four bedrooms. On the contrary, many praised the feeling of spaciousness that the cathedral ceilings would provide in the three- and four-bedroom units. (It was interesting how easily the concept was grasped from the cardboard models.) Another feature, the height of the ceilings in the bedroom units, was welcomed even though it was more difficult to visualize in model form. The height of the bedroom on the third floor was extended by allowing the finished ceiling to follow the slope of the pitched roof, and a cantilevered loft was installed for storage space, as in the starter house. There was enough headroom in the high-ceilinged bedrooms for a three-tiered bunk bed, to accommodate new family members. Or the loft floor could be extended and transformed into a sleeping area, especially since there was space above the living room floor.

During the consultations, prospective tenants often expressed concern about security, and it sometimes took a good deal of explanation to convince them that the "townhouses" were as safe, if not more so, than the locked tower. Since the entrances to the units are on short pedestrian lanes, tenants are able to observe the comings and goings in their little neighborhoods and soon get to know who belongs there. One can view the outside areas from the second- and third-floor rooms. All this attention to the exterior public and private spaces satisfied the users' need for a sense of control.

In addition, each lane can be reached directly from the street or garage by its own locked stairway. The only access to the courtyard is from the lanes or second-floor doors in the tower—strangers could not wander in—and its use as a thoroughfare is minimized by the individual entrances to low-rise sections of the project.

In fact, because all the buildings face away from the court-yard, it has the character of a large backyard, where kids living in the project or attending the day-care center can play safely and elderly tower residents can get together in the sun or, if still well-disposed toward children, can keep an eye on things. (There is also a community room in the tower for the seniors. This room has direct access to the plaza.)

This heavily used play area in the central courtyard is often watched over by elderly residents seated under the trellis.

The use of small sculptural details on a large wall surface helps break the building mass down to a human scale.

THE AESTHETICS OF DIVERSITY

While security is an important reason for locating the entrances on pedestrian lanes, a concomitant purpose is to enhance the intimacy of the dwellings and to make them feel more like individual homes than units in a project.

One of the most serious planning errors of past public housing projects was to put the common public space in the middle of a project and have the entries to the units from this common area. This design meant, in effect, that the residential unit "turned its back" to the street, creating a great loss of privacy to the tenant. The most serious harm, however, came in the form of gangs who eventually took control of the center space and therefore the resident's entry to his or her own home. The gang members could monitor a person's comings and goings, making it easy to harass them or steal from them. The Mar project avoids this planning error by taking its cues from the typical suburban street layout where houses are entered from the street side and not a centralized—potentially gang-controlled—prisonlike common area.

A stoop at the front door is a simple and inexpensive device for emphasizing each unit's separation from the common area. The fenced-off back patios also separate the private and public zones. Planters are placed in front of the units at the plaza level in front of the bedroom windows, and are supplied with a fertile compound, to enhance the unit occupant's privacy, and to allow tenants to grow some flowers or, if they wish, herbs.

Greenery is introduced into the project to help humanize the all-concrete environment. The planting shows the seasons and brings the residents closer to nature. The movement of wind fluttering the leaves when being watched from an interior space gives the observer some sense of changing weather. The green colors balance the natural with the man-made, and the planting brings a detail to the project that requires human care and thus enhances appreciation of the exterior spaces.

To make the facades of the buildings more attractive, shadow lines are introduced through the use of raised planes breaking up the fields of plaster. The shadow lines are created by the trim around the windows.

Windows are all multipaned and proportioned to be reminiscent of the traditional court homes in China, and so are the balcony doors. The designs of the trim, windows, doors, and roof are carried through for the tower, of course.

View from landscaped urban court. This court is surrounded by a building on three sides. Shown here is the Mar façade across the street. It lends closure to the urban court.

A major goal for the project (as it should be for any building) was to fit it aesthetically into the neighborhood. Because of the substantial variation in the massing (height, breadth, and width) of the surrounding structures, that was a big problem. For example, the Oakland senior-care facility across from the tower was built in 1910 and, in the fashion of the time, is elaborately massed with decorative towers and a colonnade with a detailed mixture of brick, terra-cotta, ironwork, and marble.

Budgetary restrictions made it impossible to use materials that would replicate the complex facade of the hotel (even if it were desirable to do so). But a way was found to enrich the surface of the tower so that it became a modern complement to the hotel.

As a perceptive architectural reviewer of the project, Herb Childress, explained:

> Using the most mundane of materials—stucco, aluminum, framed stock windows, iron grill . . . has made the surface come alive in an exuberant composition in which the logic of modern construction systems has become pictorial. The expansion joints for the stucco are not evenly spaced on the facade, but are placed to define the divisions of the apartments behind it; the roof gutter down spouts, rather than being "painted out," have been emphasized, their white lines helping to delineate edges and separations; even the sheet-metal vent inlets are called out in stark white and aligned up the wall, helping to direct our vision. Nothing is hidden, nothing left to chance. The face is broken into staggered vertical segments, two of which—one is the stairwell and the other is the elevator shaft—are finished in . . . earthen brown (stucco) contrasting with the sand gray of the majority of the facade and helping to break the facade into simpler, more understandable segments.[5]

The exterior design of the low-rise buildings draws on the neighborhood's Asian culture. Recessed balconies, red frames for the doors and windows of the stores, and leaf-green, steep roofs with ribbing to suggest tiles, along with the multipaned windows and balcony doors—all are features commonly found in Chinatown adaptations of Asian architectural features from a variety of sources.

On the other hand, the Mar's curved edges along the roof and curved lintels over some windows capture the form of top-story windows in some old low-rise commercial buildings across from the project. The surrounding buildings consist of a well-designed two-story government building to the east, one that has an arched colonnade facade facing our site, the eight-story brick-

Street-level commercial occupancy, three levels of residential townhouses and apartments, large exterior balconies, green-ribbed residential roof shapes, and the commercial space's red window mullions. The colors for the buildings were chosen by the owner and architect. The project's green-ribbed roofs were modeled after the roof texture of typical Chinese courthouses. The red trim around the entry doors connotes good luck according to Chinese folklore.

walled senior residents' home facing the north side (described above), and a one- and four-story arched facade facing the west side. On the south side of the complex is your typical urban infill, one-, two-, and three-story shops and offices. These elements have arched facades and small-scale features that the Mar project considered so important to pick up. The variety of the neighboring structures is suggested by alternating front and side views of the townhouses. Further variation is evident in the wall surfaces in the balcony areas, which are finished with the earthen-colored stucco used on the tower.

All in all, the Mar project is a singular example of participatory architecture. It provides private, secure, and congenial places to live, at an affordable cost, for about 300 low-income people, some of whom had actually been homeless in the sense that they had been forced to live with relatives or friends or in fleabag hotel rooms. The Mar project responds to the needs and desires of the tenants. It contributes to the redevelopment of downtown Oakland and hopefully will encourage private developers to build middle-income housing in the neighborhood, thereby enticing people who work in the area to dwell there instead of commuting from the suburbs. The variety of design elements intentionally expresses the multiplicity of cultures represented in the community by blending traditional Chinese courthouse architecture with that of a new American urban space. In 1991 the British-based Building and Social Housing Foundation named the Mar project recipient of its prestigious World Habitat Award for innovative housing.

Chapter Six

BATTLE FOR A FAIR PROCESS

The force of Nimbyism is one of the main things that is causing metropolitan regions like the [San Francisco] Bay Area and Los Angeles to erupt like volcanoes and spill over their natural boundaries of hills and out into the distant hinterlands. It is just so much easier to build where you're not in anyone's backyard. The only price is three hours on the freeway each day. Learning to deal with Nimbyism is therefore fundamental, something upon which the whole future of regions depends. To fight Nimbyism, to coop it, to sneak past it, to anesthetize it, to seduce it: any tactic is OK, except giving in.

Daniel Solomon[1]

NOT IN MY BACK YARD

Desirable though community participation in the design process may be, it sometimes leads to a furious conflict of interests. That in itself is not a bad thing. Our type of government, after all, thrives on differences of opinion. But the outcome can be decidedly undemocratic when one of the contestants is a powerful minority, supported by contingency-fee lawyers, intent on getting its own way whatever the consequences for everyone else. In the housing industry, the undemocratic obstruction usually takes the form of what has become known as "Nimbyism," meaning "Not in My Back Yard." Time and again these minority neighborhood groups have prevented the construction of affordable homes and have been responsible for the perpetuation of suburban sprawl. Rather than spend countless hours negotiating and manipulating these groups through the mandatory public hearing process, builders and their architects often shy away from a project or compromise the building design to the point that it bears little resemblance to the original concept. But when Nimbyism raised its ugly head to protest a commercial/residential mixed-use project in San Francisco designed by MacDonald Architects, the developer Richard Klein, a civic-minded local business owner, chose to fight. He mustered popular support in the community against a group of some of the wealthiest and most influential people in the city, and a no-holds-barred political battle was waged.

ORIGINS OF THE CONFLICT

The battleground was an area located in the western part of San Francisco known as the Outer Richmond. Less than a century ago it was a wasteland of fog- and wind-swept sand dunes, one of those microclimates for which San Francisco is famous. However, it is now densely built up with three- to four-story middle-income single- and two-family homes interspersed with four-story apartment buildings. The posh neighborhood in one direction is wealthy, and backs on to the magnificent 110-acre Lincoln Park, which affords incomparable views from the central hill area of the park, the Pacific Ocean, and Golden Gate.

Over the years the availability of relatively inexpensive homes and land to build on attracted various ethnic groups to the area, mainly Russians and other Eastern Europeans, Irish, and Jews. Except for some Japanese who quietly settled there when they were freed from the American concentration camps after World War II, the Outer Richmond acquired the character of a polyglot European community. Then during the 1980s an increasing number of Chinese and other Asians moved there, until by the end of the decade they constituted nearly half of the population. Like the other residents, they were mostly business people, professionals, and white-collar or skilled blue-collar workers. As a result an acute shortage of middle-income housing developed. The battle occurred because of an effort to respond to the need.

In 1984, about four years before the political turmoil connected with Klein's proposed project began, the city planning commission had designated two locations in the Outer Richmond (along with others throughout the city) as Neighborhood Commercial Shopping Center (NC-S) districts. NC-S districts were, in the words of the city's planning code, "intended to serve as shopping centers or supermarket sites which provide retail goods and services for primarily car-oriented shoppers." The major purpose of the designation was to entice people to do their shopping in the neighborhood, instead of driving to other parts of the city, thereby adding to traffic congestion and air pollution. By specifically permitting mixed commercial and residential use of buildings, as long as the former is confined to the first and second stories, NC-S zoning also furthers the city's policy of encouraging "higher residential density in areas adjacent to downtown and in neighborhood commercial districts where higher density will not have harmful effects."

Establishment of an NC-S district is always preceded by exhaustive public hearings in which everyone in the affected area is invited to participate. The local neighborhoods are notified before these hearings take place so that if they object to the NC-S designation, or the kinds of massing and uses that are likely to occur on NC-S sites, they can block the designation or modify some of the zoning terms. The process aims to get community support for new projects that may be developed for the NC-S areas so that when a new project is proposed, the project can move ahead freely, without great fanfare or unnecessary expenses. Thus if the protest groups that caused the Outer Richmond battle had challenged the NC-S designation right away, they could have saved all of the participants a lot of time, money, and effort.

One of the districts designated for the Outer Richmond NC-S zone consisted almost entirely of a site occupied by a small super-market surrounded by a large parking lot. For a variety of rea-sons—underutilization of the site, the age of the store and its obsolete building parts, an increase in the area's population of

Existing Safeway store and parking lot. The trees at the edge of the park behind the store were planted to form a visual barrier between the super-market and the park.

households, and consumers wanting greater variety in food-stuffs—the store was to be demolished and a new, enlarged store constructed to accommodate the needs of the "Nineties" consumer. It occurred to the owner of the property that his site was ideal for a mixed-use building—an expanded supermarket on the first floor, shops on the second, and residential units on the third, in accordance with one of the stated goals of NC-S zoning. Since the site was on a steep grade, the residential units would be about three stories over the grade where the site meets the corner of Lincoln Park. At the time, the border of the park was lined with luxurious trees that would provide a lovely backdrop for the homes while separating a playground and some maintenance

PLEASE COMPLETE THIS SURVEY AND RETURN IT TO THE STORE MANAGER AT 3132 CLEMENT STREET, SAN FRANCISCO. THANK YOU.

Do you shop at this store often? *Since 1953* Yes X No

If not, why? *Comment: By car – it is difficult to load bags of groceries into car when carts are not allowed to car*

How many times a week do you shop here? 1 __ 2 X 3 or more __

Do you walk to the store? Yes X No

Do you drive to the store? *occasionally* Yes X No

Do you find parking a problem at this store? Yes __ No X

Are the current store operating hours enough? Yes X No

Would you like this store open 24 hours? Yes __ No X

Are the aisles wide enough? *✱* Yes X No

Does the store carry all the items you need? Yes X No

Please check what services you would like to see:

__	Delicatessen	X	Fish Market
__	Pharmacy	X	Full-Service Floral
X	Bakery	__	Salad Bar

(Over)

✱ The aisles are wide enough if you don't pile things in the center.

What services would you like available to you in the neighborhood?

__	Shoe Repair	__	Emergency Medical Facility
X	Hardware/Paint Store	__	Dentist Office
__	Jewelry/Watch Repair/Sales	__	Optometrist
X	Stationery Store	__	Hair Salon
__	Children's Toy Store	X	Bookstore
__	Travel Agency	__	Laundromat
__	Insurance Office	__	Stereo Shop
__	Real Estate Office	__	Sporting Goods
__	Clothing/Family	__	Dry Cleaners
		X	*notions*

THANK YOU FOR COMPLETING THIS SURVEY. IF YOU WISH TO BE CONTACTED FOR FURTHER INFORMATION, PLEASE COMPLETE BELOW

(Optional) Name _____

Address _____

Phone _____

Questionnaires that were handed out at the check-out counters of the Safeway store.

A block-model massing study with the residential modules sitting on a platform above the commercial spaces. This model is purposely lacking in detail; it is used only for volumetric building-site studies.

buildings in the park from the new construction. (It should be noted that the playground was located well away from the walls of the planned project.) The second-floor shops would complement a line of existing small stores and a restaurant across the street. The supermarket owner and users enthusiastically supported the idea.

Before proceeding with the design, the owner asked the supermarket to distribute questionnaires to its shoppers asking what stores and services people would like to have in the neighborhood, as well as some questions concerning the remodeling of the supermarket's interior space. The questionnaire did not ask for responses concerning the residential segment of the program.

The residents were not asked whether they would like to see fast-food outlets incorporated into the plan, partly to avoid the suggestion of competition with existing food stores and restaurants, but mainly because such outlets produce a high volume of people and garbage, and because youngsters tend to hang out at such places. At that point, the feedback from users and the owner was fine. Customers clearly welcomed the prospect of an enlarged market and more stores in the area. Other shop owners of businesses across the street said, when interviewed, that they thought the development would be good for their business.

The results of the customer survey, along with a massing model of the project, were taken to city hall to show the planning director. Massing models show only the blocked-out, volumetric shapes, and the locations, of the buildings in a proposed project. They show no details, such as windows, doors, roof shapes, etc. Such models are shown only to planners, architects, and clients. A layman viewing a model in this state might erroneously view it

A highly detailed architectural model of the proposed project. This model was developed to help the layman visualize the building in three dimensions and gain a sense of how it might visually impact the community. Using an architectural model in public hearings often clears up misunderstandings and speeds up the acceptance of infill projects.

as the real thing, which might lead him to reject a different kind of model in the later stages of project development.

The city hall planning director said it looked all right to him because it followed the approved NC-S zoning guidlines without exception.

Since it is difficult for laymen to visualize a building from architectural drawings, a more highly detailed and colored model was built showing what the project would look like according to the architect's preliminary design. The model included shapes, windows, entrances, colors, landscaping, and other details depicting the architectural context that exists within one city block of the site. A series of meetings was then held at the supermarket with groups of neighboring homeowners, shopkeepers, and other concerned people within a 300-foot radius of the site. (Before construction begins on a new project, the San Francisco Planning Department notifies all property owners within a 300-foot radius of the construction site.) Everyone was invited and many attended.

Attendees were shown the model plans of each building level and drawings of the four sides of the project, and were asked to express any concerns and make suggestions. A number were intrigued and a few dismayed by the various shapes and pastel colors of the residential units and facades of the second-floor shops. But when explanations were provided about how they reflected the colors and shapes of the surrounding homes and other buildings, the design won general approval.

A representative of an Asian community association suggested the inclusion of a community meeting room (and in later drawings one was added). Residents of homes adjacent to the

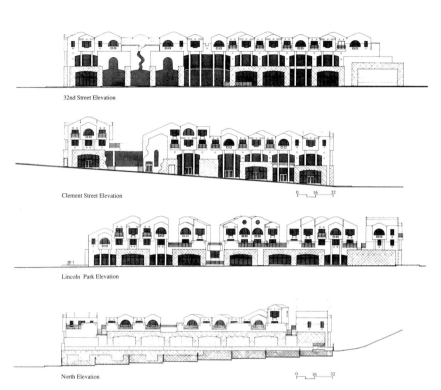

32nd Street Elevation

Clement Street Elevation

Lincoln Park Elevation

North Elevation

Proposed building elevations. [From top] A: Entry for automobiles is at left, in the center for pedestrians, and at right for unloading trucks. B: The first stepped level consists of commercial spaces, the second level is a shopping arcade, and the third contains residential units. On the left side of the elevation and above the supermarket is the entry to the shopping mart. C: Three-story elevation facing Lincoln Park. The first level is commercial, with two-level residential townhouses above. D: North elevation facing the backyards of single-family homes. It shows one story of residential units over one story of commercial units. The foundation line along this elevation is stepped to match the backyards of the adjacent homes.

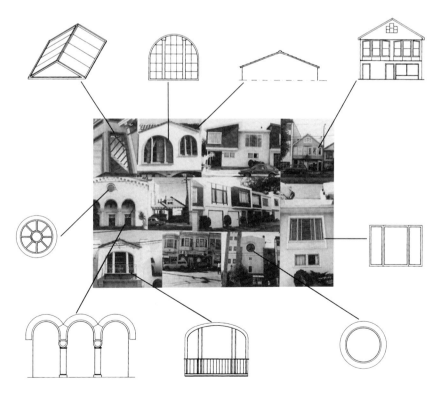

Elements of local architectural vocabulary that were used as cues in the architectural design of the new project. The arches, pitched roofs, and window shapes are evident in the four preceding elevations.

north side of the site were concerned about shadows cast by the building. A shadow study was conducted by MacDonald Architects, and information from the study was used to modify the building edge to reduce the shadows that would affect back-yards and windows in ground-floor rooms. Other suggestions were minor and mostly concerned the types of stores to be included. No outright opposition to the project was expressed at any of the meetings. Indeed, there was general approbation.

Ordinarily, the next step in the approval process would be a formal application for a building site permit and public hearings by the planning department. But because public hearings were customarily held in the city center, away from the concerned com-munity which for the most part works during the day, it was decided to hold a mock public hearing in the evening at the com-munity church, using the guidelines for a standard planning department hearing. This would satisfy the owner, who wanted the community to be fully represented, and allow neighborhood residents to express their concerns about the new project in their midst. The San Francisco Planning Department cooperated in this hearing and was kind enough to have a representative present to answer questions from the audience.

THE ATTACK IS LAUNCHED

Among the forty or so people who attended the mock hearing were some Sea Cliff residents. Sea Cliff is a wealthy neighbor-hood that begins about a quarter of a mile from the project site and extends northward to the ocean. Many of its expensive homes overlook the sea to the north where it enters the Golden Gate into San Francisco Bay. As a rule, these residents did not shop at the run-down supermarket on the project site, but drove more than two miles to an upscale shopping center in another district. At the meeting they, as well as others, asked trenchant questions about parking, the height of the building, traffic impacts, control of teenagers who use the adjacent park at night, and other matters. Although some people were obviously con-cerned about the project, the audience seemed to have a generally favorable view of the drawings and models and to agree with the survey results. The meeting was amicable, and there were no arguments to speak of.

When the owner applied for a site building permit, however, he was challenged. A group of Sea Cliff residents calling itself the

Lincoln Park Neighborhood Association demanded a full-scale third-party environmental impact report (EIR) covering everything from the effects of the project on traffic and transportation facilities to shadows cast and hazardous materials produced, even though the planning department felt that it was not needed. This group of about fifty homes occupied both sides of one long city block and in the past had formed to stop the expansion of a girls' school that backed on their backyards. The supermarket project was two blocks away. Although EIRs are expensive, and are rarely required for such a small building project, the owner acquiesced, both to keep the peace and to protect himself in case of lengthy litigation. (It is at this point in the project development that the opposition has the opportunity to circumvent the majority wishes by appealing all aspects of the draft EIR, slowing the project, or even preventing it from seeing the light of day.)

Then the Association launched an attack. It distributed a scurrilous leaflet throughout the area. Headlined "!!! SAVE YOUR NEIGHBORHOOD!!!" the leaflet warned, in English and Chinese:

> A Developer is trying to tear down the Safeway store at Clement Street and 32nd Avenue, and build a Monstrous Building— *324,000 square feet and seven levels.* Two levels underground parking, three levels retail space (about the same size as Laurel Village Shopping Center), and two levels of 77 single unit apartments. This is a *Downtown size* mixed-use district shopping mall that will devastate our neighborhood. It will destroy the adjacent Lincoln Park Views and cast a shadow over the playground. Initial calculations show that up to 4000 people could visit the site each day, and generate over *5000 one-way auto trips—A 1000% INCREASE.* The existing 40 foot wide streets cannot handle that traffic. It is also calculated that there could be a *shortfall of over 100 parking spaces.* Those cars will park on neighborhood streets!

Most of the statements were false, as the EIR later verified. First of all, the leaflet implied that the supermarket would be torn down permanently, which of course was not true. The existing 18,100-square-foot store would be replaced with one almost twice as large—35,500 square feet—the minimum size for a single store needed to market the wide variety of products that the modern consumer demands. A smaller store would not be profitable, and most supermarkets today average 50,000 to 60,000 square feet. The figure of 324,000 total square footage was about right (actually it would be 330,900 square feet), but the way it was stated gave the impression that the building would cover

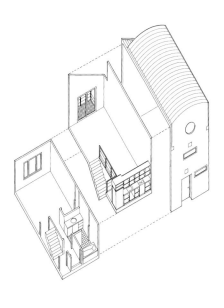

Axonometric of a proposed two-story one-bedroom townhouse. The living-dining room is upstairs and the bedroom is downstairs.

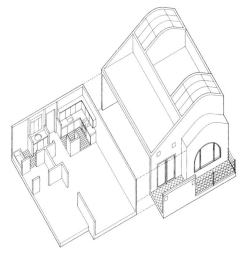

Axonometric of a proposed one-bedroom apartment with a high ceiling and skylight over the living room and kitchen.

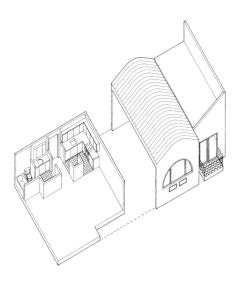

Axonometric of a proposed studio apartment with an outside cantilevered deck.

324,000 square feet of land—impossible on a 72,000-square-foot site. The building would have six levels, not seven: two for underground parking, one for the supermarket and one above it for shops, and two for the housing.

In fact, the second housing level was only partial, since it comprised the upper floor of thirty-four two-story townhouses, out of a total of seventy-four units, not seventy. All the other units, consisting of seventeen one-bedroom cottage-type homes and twenty-three studio flats (similar to the starter homes), were one story high.

The assertion that the housing would consist of "single-unit apartments" was obviously false, and as to the statement about destroying views from the adjacent section of Lincoln Park, the leaflet failed to mention that a line of luxuriously foliated trees already blocked the horizontal views. This blocking of views from the perimeters of the park was done on purpose because the original designers of urban parks used the trees to completely separate the urban context from the park. The intention was presumably to allow one to escape city life by entering a "rural" setting free of city structures. (Mysteriously, the trees were pruned of their lower branches shortly after the homeowners' leaflet appeared.) The 40-foot-high building (the limit for NC-S zoning) would not interfere with views from higher elevations of the park any more than an existing four-story apartment building across the street from the project. No shadows from the building would be cast on the playground. The "calculations" about the people who would visit the site in the course of a day, the auto trips to the neighborhood, and the shortfall of parking spaces were scare tactics. Granted, there would be an increase in trips—about fifteen percent a day—but a large portion would be to the expanded supermarket, which no one objected to. And during the evening rush hour, only about 655 new person-trips would be generated, of which 410 would be by car, 50 by public transportation, and 200 on foot. The EIR had this to say about the project's impact on traffic patterns and parking:

> The project would remove approximately 125 [current] parking spaces and would construct 297. Projected parking demand would be for about 245 spaces. The City Planning Code would require the project to provide 225 spaces. The project would create an on-site surplus over demand. Because the project would provide excess parking spaces on-site, no parking impacts are expected on local streets. The 50 [public transportation] person-trips the project would generate in the p.m. peak hour would add less than one

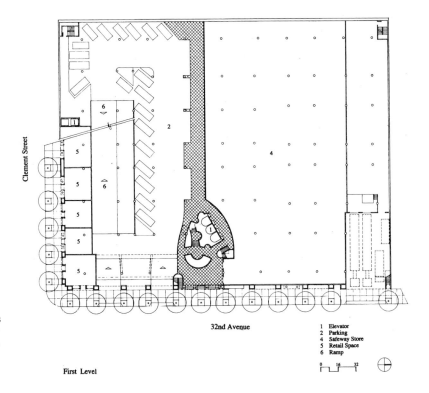

The grade-level functions along 32nd Avenue. To the right are the loading docks and to the left is the entry to the supermarket, under which there are two complete levels of parking.

Clement Street

6

2

5

5

6

5

5

4

5

5

1

32nd Avenue

1 Elevator
2 Parking
4 Safeway Store
5 Retail Space
6 Ramp

0   16   32

First Level

passenger to each of the buses available during that period on the eight routes within three blocks of the site.[2]

The findings of the EIR were predictable. Indeed, the parking problem had been studied very carefully for the design of the project, and greatly improved truck loading facilities had been provided for the new supermarket.

The leaflet was just the beginning. For presentations to community groups and city officials, the Association had an architect draw a picture purportedly showing what the project would look like when built.

Distorted perspective made the building look 50 percent higher than it would be and more massive, as if it would loom over the neighborhood, whereas it was actually no higher than the apartment buildings across the street. Streets were depicted as narrow, and cars and a bus were drawn in to suggest congestion. Street landscaping was omitted.

Mounting a full-scale campaign, the Association hired a lawyer, whose practice—ironically—consisted primarily of representing developers. The first step of a legal battle centered on a 1952 planning department stipulation on the supermarket's construction permit that the building cover no more than twenty-five percent of the site. Since the community-approved NC-S designation implicitly nullified that stipulation, and no objections had been raised to the NC-S rezoning of Outer Richmond, it would take a naive lawyer indeed to think he could successfully maintain retention of the restriction. Indeed, throughout the city similar stipulations had been removed as a matter of course as new building types were created and rezoning took place. However, an exceptionally cool reception of the owner's representations at city hall led him to believe that the Association was not relying on legal proceedings alone, but was also using the not-inconsiderable inside influence of its members to place obstacles in the way of the project. Nasty statements to the press and letters to the editor further raised the temperature of the campaign.

COUNTERATTACK

Bewildered by the ferocity of the attack, the owner and his associates corrected the misrepresentations in interviews with the press, letters to the editor, and documents submitted to city officials. But, as so often happens, facts and reason seemed to drown in sensationalist propaganda. To muster popular support for the project, the owner circulated a petition depicting the program in detail and requesting that the city approve it. This leaflet was distributed throughout the area where the users of the supermarket lived; the perimeters of the area of distribution were determined by pinpointing the locations of the addresses on the responses to the first community-impact survey.

More than 5000 people signed the petition. A map showing where they lived demonstrated that an overwhelming majority of the people in the mostly middle-income sections of the area favored the project and that major opposition was confined to the small enclaves of the wealthy.

The owner offered to meet with the members of the Association to discuss how the project might be modified to make it more acceptable to them. At each meeting, however, the Association demanded more concessions, and it became clear that this was merely a diversionary tactic; what they really wanted was to stop the project completely. Eventually, the Association offered two alternative proposals. One retained the stipulation that the supermarket occupy no more than twenty-five percent of the site while including thirty-two rental units on top of it. Because this supermarket would actually be smaller than the current one, the proposed plan was not profitable. The Association had to have known that the supermarket people would not buy that idea. The other proposal involved dividing the site into two lots, one for a larger supermarket and the other for a conventional thirty-one-unit apartment building. This alternative was unrealistic because it did not comply with San Francisco's planning codes, which require every project to provide sufficient parking for the project's intended users.

As a compromise, the owner reluctantly offered to reduce the size of the project to three floors: the first and a mezzanine to contain a 35,555-square-foot market and 17,000 square feet of other retail space, and the second and third to be devoted to forty-nine residential units—a large reduction from the originally proposed seventy-four. Parking for the supermarket would be underground. One residential parking space per unit would be on top of the supermarket roof, accessed by a ramp from the street. Commercial parking and residential parking would be entirely separate. The Association's proposals were unrealistic to the supermarket and unbuildable to the owner; the owner's offer was unacceptable to the Association. A stalemate was reached. A supermarket chain that later optioned the land from the owner is currently trying to bring the project—albeit much altered from its original design—to fruition. The opposition continues to be well organized, and it will be another three to four years more until the project is realized.

THE ISSUE OF HIGH-DENSITY DEVELOPMENT

In the early stages of the battle, it was hard to understand why the Association was so frantic in its opposition. The building would not change the architectural character of the neighborhood in any significant way. Already a number of apartment buildings existed nearby with greater density than this project, and many structures in the area contained residential units over retail space. The small Association had not opposed the NC-S designation in its earlier public hearings. True, the project would be somewhat larger than some buildings in the area, but not so much as to be called "monstrous." As the conflict progressed, however, there were indications of hidden motives. A key to the Association's true sentiments was a rhetorical question asked at the mock public hearing: "Would the project lead to further development in the neighborhood?" Then in a form letter circulated to residents, soliciting financial support for the lawyer's fees (reportedly $100,000), there was a revealing statement. The letter warned that the increased number of people the project would attract to the neighborhood would "bring the 'C word'—crime—to dangerous levels. The present relative safety of even taking a walk will be gone." For a clincher the letter added that "a definite downward impact on the property values in the neighborhood" would result. Undoubtedly, the epistle was meant to frighten residents, and perhaps the authors were genuinely frightened themselves. But clearly the concern was deeper. The project threatened a few homeowners' perception of the Outer Richmond as a suburban haven. It would, the letter insisted, "create a real mini-Manhattan directly next to Lincoln Park."

That was the issue. The project itself was not the problem, but that it would open the way to more development in the district. Understandably, perhaps, residents of fine homes worried about the encroachment of the city on their Camelot. In that regard, they were like residents of many other neighborhoods—wealthy ones especially, but also some composed of middle-income private homes. And the opposite has also occurred. Residents of low-income areas have attempted to prevent development in some instances because they were afraid of losing their homes, or of rent increases, as a result of gentrification.

But what is the alternative? Housing is desperately needed, and more will be required as the population continues to grow. Further suburban sprawl is not acceptable. The health and environmental costs of the resulting air pollution, consumption of energy, depletion and contamination of water resources, the use of grade-one flat agricultural land, and the destruction of forests are much too high. Air pollution, for example, has been blamed for more than 53,000 deaths a year in the United States and for $40 to $50 billion annually in health care costs and lost work.[3] One study of the San Francisco area showed that suburbanites drive four times as many miles as apartment dwellers in the city, and that suburban single-family homes occupy forty times more land, require forty times more lumber when constructed, and use much more water and fuel than the same number of units in urban multifamily buildings.[4] The coexisting problems of not enough housing and rising taxes will not be solved by a continuation of spread-out development patterns. Our existing cities have many vacant and underutilized lots with infrastructure in place, and like it or not, growth has to be confined as much as possible to infill areas—both in cities and in extant suburbs—that have already been developed. We must refurbish our cities and make them livable. The study recommended mixed-use residential/commercial development as the most desirable type of housing from the environmental point of view, mainly because people do not have to jump in their cars every time they want to go to the store. And construction of a mixed-use building on a site that is already occupied by a one-story structure like the supermarket is a very efficient way to grow. Wasted air space is utilized for the housing.

In the conflict over the Outer Richmond, as in other, similar conflicts, the basic issue was fairness. The question was, Could a small elitist group block a high-density development, which was designed in accordance with preapproved guidelines and zoning requirements, and met the demand for homes without causing unnecessary damage to the environment? This is not to suggest that residents of a neighborhood do not have the right to a say in what will be built in their backyards. But residents of the Outer Richmond *did* have a say at the time the site was zoned NC-S for mixed use, and they *did* have a say when a 40-feet height limit was set on new construction. Once an agreement has been reached through an established zoning hearing process, and once contradictory points of view have been aired and a solution agreed upon by consensus of majority rule, developers should be able to proceed without fear of undue obstruction and the resultant expense. Objections might be raised to design elements and details, and the developer has the obligation to respond. Fundamentals, though, should no longer be in dispute. Unfortunately, Nimbyists often disregard and abuse the democratic process. As a result, the environment suffers or housing is not built. Developers, too, are at fault. To circumvent the political turmoil that all too often accompanies infill development, they give up without a fight. They build in areas where political issues do not arise, creating ever more suburban towns.

Chapter Seven

THE SUBURBAN VILLAGE

Decentralization feeds on raw land, which is certainly not in end-less supply. For circulation, it relies largely on the automobile, whose roads and highways are becoming increasingly clogged, whose emissions are mostly responsible for the brown haze filling our skies, and whose fuel is expected to dwindle within the next thirty to forty years. . . . It promotes social and political division, often separating people by class or race, and dispersing political power to the point where people sharing common interests . . . find it difficult, if not impossible, to work with one another.

Greenbelt Alliance[1]

"THE NEW TOWN"

One of the latest architectural abominations is a type of suburban development called "the new town." The best-known example is Seaside, an eighty-acre community built from scratch along 2300 feet of oceanfront on Florida's Gulf Coast.

Aside from its prime seashore location, the site afforded the developer a major undemocratic advantage: It was in an unincorporated area, so the developer was free of public participation in the planning process and unencumbered by city planning codes. The developer and land planner could do pretty much what they wanted to do without the usual public input. Their contempt for democracy is shown by a set of rigid zoning and building codes they adopted for the construction of new homes on the property. These codes included specifications for allowable styles, the depth

The low housing density and the lack of urban scale cause this rural development to be just another piece of suburban sprawl.

of front yards, the height and pitch of the roof, and fence designs. Seaside is one development team's opinion of how we should live in a community.

Moreover, a grid pattern for the streets lined up the buildings like soldiers on parade. And the houses had to have front porches—on which, presumably, residents loll in rocking chairs on balmy evenings, keeping an eye on the comings and goings of their neighbors. The developer wanted to recreate the atmosphere of a small southern town from the horse-and-buggy days, and succeeded in doing so with all the stultifying homogeneity.[2]

The American Institute of Architects has acclaimed Seaside and developments like it as the "suburbs of the future." But more suburbs are precisely what we do not need. We do not (or at least should not) want less flat farm land, more countryside destroyed, more beach shut off from the public by private development, and more economic waste as a result of the addition of unnecessary infrastructure. Since the communities are usually built on the outskirts of previous suburban development, residents have to drive a longer distance to work if their jobs are in the city, increasing the air pollution and congestion. At Seaside they even have to drive to the grocery and other stores, which are confined to a central "downtown." As John Field, F.A.I.A.,[3] points out:

> Seaside is only one more subdivision on the landscape, spread out low and wide, quite separate from an adequate base of jobs and shopping. Most significantly, it is impractical and unaffordable for most Americans, even though it is appealing in the same way that a home furnishings store window is. Seaside is essentially yet one more elitist concept for housing in the long line of so-called "innovations.". . . Americans will have to create . . . new patterns of development in order to achieve more functional, more livable, and more human metropolitan living—making use of concepts that include rather than ignore the given realities of our cities and suburbs.[4]

SUBURBAN NO-MAN'S-LAND

Until construction of a high-speed freeway along the shore of San Francisco Bay after World War II, the main artery between San Francisco and San Jose fifty miles to the south was a boulevard called El Camino Real. It used to run past miles of flat countryside consisting of orchards and cropland, but gradually the trees were felled and the ground bulldozed to make way for suburbs. The boulevard itself became a commercial strip, mostly one lot deep. Lots behind it were undesirable for residential or commercial use and were therefore largely underdeveloped. Similar no-man's-lands between commercial and residential zones exist in most suburbs, and they are ripe for development.

In the early 1980s two innovative developers, Alexander Kulakoff and Walter Harrington, asked MacDonald Architects to design a combined commercial and residential condominium project on a four-acre site along El Camino Real, in the bedroom community of Mountain View, a city near the center of the electronics industry located between San Francisco and San Jose. At the time the west side of the site along El Camino Real was zoned for commercial use, and the single-family detached homes facing the east side were zoned for residential use. The initial idea, therefore, was to build residential space next to commercial space.

As we talked we came to the conclusion that rather than separate the functions we would integrate them, creating a kind of Southwest Indian pueblo-type village, with stores on the ground floor and the residences above. A project like that had not been built in an American suburban context for a long time, and it took a particularly sensitive Mountain View planning staff to allow us to introduce three-dimensional zoning for commercial and residential use. Zoning in the United States is almost always two-dimensional—east-west and north-south. Only recently have cities begun to make an effort to accommodate three-dimensional zoning. Now the Mountain View officials had to zone vertical, as well as horizontal, space. They had to think differently.

I explained my village concept to the city planners with a block model, and once they understood our intentions of a more sophisticated way of zoning, they helped us achieve the built results.

For the actual design, I drew less on European examples than on an indigenous American one, the pueblo. I had long been intrigued by the villages built by native Americans in northern New Mexico, especially the Hopi pueblo at Taos. The pueblo as a housing structure has been continuously occupied over 1000 years. Therefore I felt it would be an excellent example to study as a living, changing, and workable structure for human habitation. The pueblo Indians' basic system of creating and using building spaces presents a very simple ideal that spiritually and physically works with the natural environment. For the pueblo model to work as well as it has for such a long time the structure had to be flexible and easily added to. It had to have interior and exterior spaces that were adequate to raise a family in—spaces for cooking, cleaning, festivals, and security—and structured for traditional tribal activities—the same basic elements that go into good planning at any time.

Taos, and other pueblos too, seemed to me to have a unique power, a driving force very unlike the refined impact of most European architecture. The power was primitive perhaps, born of nature and part of it, but for that very reason liberating. In building their homes, the Hopi were unrestricted by abstract notions about style, form, and detailing. Traditional architectural terms do not even apply. The builders' concepts were shaped only by their environment, their needs, and the readily available building materials, which were pine logs and riverbed clays.

The Taos Pueblo Catholic Church was built using the same construction method and materials used for construction of a typical pueblo. This form of church construction is not prevalent in other communities outside of New Mexico's pueblos. In those communities the early Catholic churches are usually built of masonry blocks, and are monumental in scale.

Taos blends into the hovering mountains, with its structures reflecting their rugged shape. The profound difference from traditional European architecture is illustrated by the pueblo's church. As architectural historian Vincent Scully points out:

> The church stands up facing the mountain . . . but here, as in all the pueblos, the old harmonic twin-towered facade of Western European church architecture is pulled into gentler undulations of outline to suggest rather than to oppose the mountain's form. . . . There is a clear contrast here with the church of San Francisco de Taos, which serves the Spanish community just down the valley . . . . Its towers are aggressively European . . . and they challenge the mountains with considerable machismo, but the pueblo will not permit its church to do so. It is not interested in heroic confrontation but in cooperative interplay.[5]

That "cooperative interplay" with nature expresses the spirit of a truly American architecture, a strong free-flowing architecture rooted in a gloriously diverse and fecund land—which unhappily has been overlaid with the oppressive formality of grids, "harmonious" (that is, following classical goals of perfection) towers, and endless sameness.

Taos Pueblo comprised a dozen or so structures, ranging in size from one story to five, clustered on both sides of Taos Creek

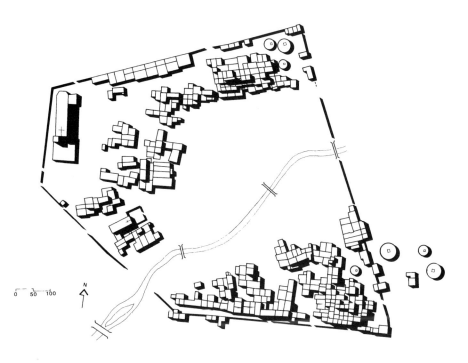

Site plan of the Taos Pueblo, with Taos Creek running through its center. The seemingly random massing on the site creates a vital three-dimensional visual pattern through the interplay of shadow and light on the building mass. This informal, fragmentary massing pattern will preserve the overall aesthetics of the Pueblo, no matter how much change and volume expansion take place.

without any discernible pattern other than a vague semicircle. No grid there, not even streets as we know them, just space between the buildings. The topography, landscape, or just convenience dictated where a structure would be built. A multistory building consisted of a conglomeration of rectangular rooms (for example, 12 feet x 14 feet and 7 feet high). Those on the ground floor would ordinarily be devoted to storage, while on the upper stories some would be for sleeping and others for cooking.

The division of functions was never rigid. Sleeping rooms might be placed on the ground floor along with storage units. A cooking room might also serve for sleeping. Materials were gathered from what the land offered—adobe, rock, brush, grass, limestone for whitewash, twigs, and timber for beams—although the wood often had to be fetched from some distance away because of the scarcity of trees in the arid region. Everyone in the clan, including women, worked on the construction. The building was never really completed, because a room or two might be added when a couple married or when more space was needed for some other reason. The pueblo was alive, a genuine expression of the people who lived in it, at one with the environment from which it emerged. There were no palaces for tribal leaders, no elaborate decorations to set them aside. Empirical, egalitarian, flexible, guileless, the pueblo was perhaps the most democratic form of architecture in the world.

Applied to the Mountain View project, which Alex Kulakoff named Two Worlds, the pueblo was an inspiration for two major aspects of the design, the overall layout—that is, the massing of square cubicles—and the relationship between commercial and residential functions. Forty-odd trees grew on the Mountain View site, including some magnificent old oak, fir, and eucalyptus. Instead of uprooting them—the usual practice—we broke the project up into separate buildings and clustered them in irregularly shaped islands that weaved around the heritage-type trees. [6] With the help of the landscape architect Leslie Baronian, I managed to save all but a few. Like the builders of the pueblos, I let the site determine the massing. I completely rejected the traditional grid.

The "islands" closest to El Camino Real were true mixed-use components, with space for offices, stores, parking, and restaurants on the ground floor and two-story townhouses above. A major problem with such projects is how to prevent the commercial activity from impinging upon the homes, and here too

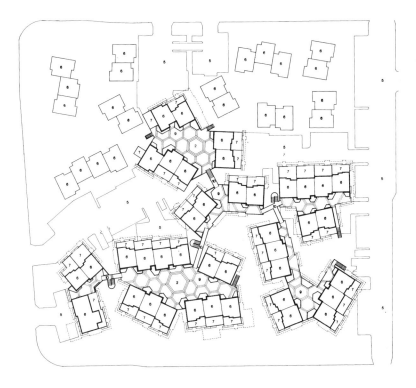

1 COMMERCIAL
2 PLANTED AREA
3 COVERED PARKING
4 WALKWAY
5 PARKING
6 RESIDENTIAL
7 PRIVATE YARD
8 BIKE PATH
9 PLAZA
10 BRIDGE

Site plan showing the layout of the townhouse units that are above parking and commercial spaces. The houses at the top of the illustration are on grade. This picks up the fragmentary context of the massing seen in the Taos Pueblo site plan. Each house has its own exterior entry and private and enclosed yard.

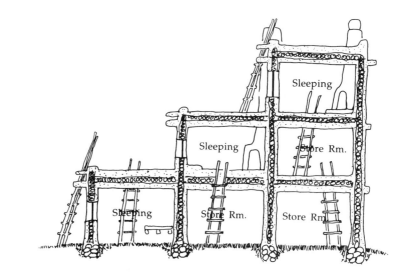

Explanatory cross section of a segment of the Taos Pueblo structure. The sleeping rooms are all on the outer areas where there is easy access to light and ventilation. The storerooms are in low-sun-light, low-ventilation areas. These interior spaces might also be used as workshops.

Building cross section through the mixed-use Two Worlds complex shows on the first level a covered colonnade adjacent and parallel to retail commercial space. On the second level there is a yard above the colonnade and a living-dining room above the retail space. On the third level are the bedrooms with exterior decks and views. There is a continuous landscape buffer at grade between the road system and the building facades.

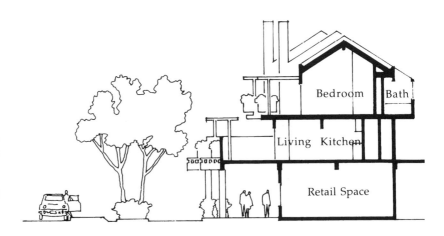

Taos Pueblo offered a solution. I adopted the terraced profile of multistory pueblo structures.

The ground-floor commercial space was roofed with a concrete platform that extended beyond the building to form a colonnaded walkway in front of the stores and a sheltered parking area in back. On top of the store, the front extension of the slab served as a passageway to the homes and the back extension as a deck off of the townhouse lower floor, which could be used for a garden for growing herbs or for flowers in planters. The second story of the house was set back farther and had a recessed balcony in front.

As a result of the terracing of the building mass, the commercial and residential elements of the building were effectively

First-level retail commercial area with the townhouses above. The owners of these condominiumized commercial spaces were encouraged to construct individualized storefronts, creating visual interest along the public walkway.

separated. There really were two worlds. The world below the concrete platform was not unlike some other well-appointed suburban shopping centers, although much more attractive because the stores were grouped around landscaped plazas on the ground level islands.

For structural and marketing reasons, we structured the commercial space of concrete in twenty-four-foot increments. The distribution of the load-bearing walls, as well as the material itself, provided very efficient support for the platform townhouses and structural parking. The dimension of the twenty-four-foot module allowed flexibility in the other dimension. One module was just right for a two-room office or small store, two modules accommodated four offices, and the depth of the unit

Custom green tile roofs were chosen to match the color of the oak tree leaves. The cedar wood trellises and planters were also introduced to carry the flora into the concrete stuccoed spaces. The trellises and stucco walls were placed in a way that enhances privacy.

from the front door to the back could also be adjusted to meet the needs of different users.

In contrast, the world above was like a quiet walled Mediterranean hillside village (an image we emphasized by means of white stucco facades that bounce light around to create the sense of more space). Cedar trellises and oak-leaf-green tiled roofs extended the sylvan milieu created by the trees. Just setting the homes back from the street distinguished them visually from the ground-level part of the building, and a parapet wall with planters on the outside of the pathway hid the entrances from view. Residents sitting on their balconies looked over planters to see treetops and the sky instead of shoppers, and their privacy was enhanced by fences, planters, and the trellises all situated to block the line of sight from any unwanted onlookers. The extended street-level platforms themselves served as efficient fire and sound barriers.

Because of the structural support provided by the columns on the ground floor and the even distribution of the strength by the platform, we were able to position the relatively lightweight wood-frame townhouses more or less the way we wanted to. Had the townhouses been one story higher we would have had to use a beam system to carry the extra loads they would have generated. My experience in designing residential buildings had convinced me that the great majority of people want a detached house, a place that's entirely their own with two internal privacy zones such as a two-level home that allows a space for children's play and an area specificaly for adults, offering relative seclusion. Separating each unit was not economically feasible. We did, however, limit the number of units in an enclave to no more than four. Also, by staggering the townhouses in two-foot increments and providing each with its own entrance, roof, chimney, and balcony, we created the illusion that the houses are detached.

Visual privacy was increased by juxtaposing the buildings at angles, so that residents would not look directly into each other's windows. As a result, the buildings were arranged in a free-form cluster around a small garden area.

The landscaping design not only made the plaza more attractive, but also made it seem larger because the massing of the building forms and their walkways was not parallel to the landscaped areas. This method of using space to increase the perspective of space when placed at ever diminishing angles is seen throughout

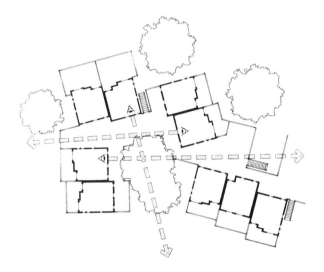

Typical housing cluster around an internal court showing the natural view lines that resulted from careful planning of the interior spaces.

Small garden area centered in the courtyard of six townhouses. Under this garden area is a submerged parking structure. Note the individual entry door to each townhouse.

the plan. A little community area was thereby formed. Its residents would spot intruders. Their space was defensible.

The terracing and the irregular clustering produced ever-changing patterns of light and shadow—a phenomenon observed, incidentally, at Taos Pueblo. To a certain extent, the effect was created deliberately. I had specified clear natural cedar for the trellises, in contrast to the white facades of the buildings, to make the balconies appear more withdrawn and private. And I knew, as every architect does of course, how light affects forms, how hues subtly change as the sun moves across the sky in the course of a day and over seasons. But there was no way to formally plan the amazing variety that actually resulted, other than to facilitate it by not lining the buildings up in a row. Here, too, was a blending with nature, a "balance between the natural and the man-made," to borrow Scully's comment on Taos.

Of the sixty-two townhouses in Two Worlds, twenty-two were not combined with commercial space so that there would be a stepped transition to the neighborhood of modest homes to the east of the site. Those nearest the mixed-use section were built atop carports six feet off of the grade, while the rest were at grade. Thus the height descended gradually from ten feet above grade to the top of the concrete platform above the commercial space, to six feet of the middle residential platform, and then to

Clustering of large family housing units around oak tree. The privacy wall of the center unit fences in a private yard that looks out on playground equipment. The massing for these houses correlates in size to the single-family detached houses across the street.

View of site showing pedestrian circulation in the dark shade and vehicular circulation in white. Note that the pedestrian circulation steps over the vehicular road and the parking system.

residential units on grade. Neighbors were delighted with the result. Instead of imposing upon their residential environment, the project served as a visual and acoustical buffer between them and the commercial zone on El Camino Real.

From one end of the site to the other, pedestrian areas were separated completely from automobile traffic. Residential levels of the islands were connected by bridges and walkways stepped down to the clusters of homes built on grade. A mother living in the farthest house to the east could send her offspring to a store on the west without the child ever having to walk across a street. Or she could wheel a baby carriage safely along wooded paths near her home. In designing the project I was determined to provide as much open space as possible for landscaping and strolling to help create the atmosphere of a village. One way was to minimize the area devoted to parking. Mountain View's building codes required four parking stalls for every 1000 square feet of commercial space, and two for every dwelling unit. To reduce the required total area of parking, I specified one covered stall for each townhouse, tucking it away in back or under the building, and mixed the rest with those needed by the store. Half the project—that is two acres out of the four—consisted of landscape, plazas, and pathways.

Two Worlds was an immediate success. Every commercial unit and all but two of the residential ones were sold within about six months. The concept of the suburban village, of people working and living at the same location, was validated. Some of the owners of the commercial condominiums also bought townhouses. Reluctance to intrude upon their privacy inhibited me from asking them exactly how many miles and hours of driving they saved every week. Under normal traffic conditions, the usual one-way commute from this Mountain View location to the centers of work such as San Jose and other surrounding cities is a twenty- to forty-mile drive.

In reviewing Two Worlds after it was built, and with the added experience I gained later from designing a similar development for a twelve-acre site in the center of Pleasant Hill, California, I formulated some guidelines for the successful construction of suburban mixed-use projects:

FINANCING. Since banks tend to view commercial space as financially riskier than housing, the proceeds from housing sales should be high enough to repay the entire construction loan. At Mountain View the commercial floor was 20,000 square feet versus 81,000 square feet of residential floor area, which is about a one-to-four ratio. The ratio of commercial to residential use was approximately the same at Two Worlds Pleasant Hill.

SITE PLANNING. Every effort should be made to preserve natural features of the site—trees, hillocks, rocks, or best of all a stream. The sun, wind, precipitation, topography, and preservation efforts determine where the structures should go. A typical city block may be required to allow a mix of usable open space (such as decks and courtyards), landscaping, and building area, thereby creating a sense of community.

COMMERCIAL SPACE. We had arrived at the twenty-four-foot-wide spacing of structural elements for the commercial space and parking stalls after consultation with realtors. It proved to be ideal, not only at Two Worlds Mountain View but also at Two Worlds Pleasant Hill.

RESIDENTIAL UNITS. While the residential units at Mountain View were not detached, the irregular clustering and individualized details created a visual sense of separation. Clustering the units around plazas gained the economic advantage of high-density development—the savings on infrastructure—but without the cold, impersonal squared-off grid that usually goes along with multiunit developments. The number of units enclosing a plaza should be limited (ideally, no more than fifteen); if there are too many units, the very sense of community and security that clustering is designed to foster will be diminished. The width of townhouses should be such that they can, when necessary, be lined up with commercial and parking stall areas.

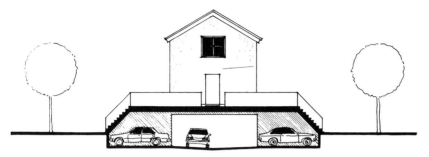

Section showing a town-house and platform over a suburban municipally-owned eighty-foot right of way. The parking for such houses would be under the platform on the sides of the four-foot recessed roadway.

PLATFORMING SUBURBAN STREETS

The platform separating the commercial and residential space is the key to another type of suburban housing development. It might be called platforming. Every suburb, almost without exception, has at least one shopping center. Ordinarily, it sprawls over the equivalent of a city block or two and consists of a group of centrally located one- or two-story buildings surrounded by a large parking lot. Everything, such as stores, offices, food center, entertainment, and promenade areas, is in place for a suburban village except the homes.

Since such a site has already been cleared and paid for and has an infrastructure in place, at relatively little expense a concrete or steel-and-concrete platform could be laid over the parking lot, with wood-frame townhouses similar to those at Two Worlds built on top. The cost to each new housing unit for its part of the platform would be about equal to the price of an on-grade residential lot of the same size.

Similarly, low-rise office buildings and light industrial plants could be transformed for mixed use by platforming over their extensive parking lots. Many of the business parks that sprang up throughout suburbia in the 1970s and 1980s are ideal candidates. Employees would not have to drive to to work, but instead just run down the stairs or walk over a bridge. In fact, a small grocery and other stores might be built at ground level to create a village-like community.

Among the realities that have to be faced are the increasing number of people who need homes, and the fact that for one reason or another a great many of them want to live in the suburbs. They have a right to do so, just as those who prefer urban life

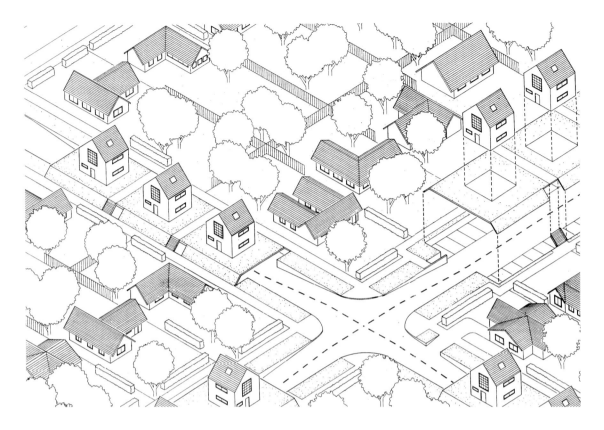

A platformed suburban street. The only visible road area is at the corner of the blocks. The parking for the existing detached suburban housing would be in the city right of way. According to the user's preference, a stall can be open or enclosed.

should be able to find affordable homes in the city. But new suburbs are not the way, particularly not elitist "new towns." The only sensible method to provide the housing is infill development of existing suburbs, old, underused light-industrial sites, and unused military bases. In many cases there is plenty of room for growth without significantly changing the character of existing residential neighborhoods. In fact, there is the chance of creating new medium-density neighborhoods within existing developed suburban areas.

As the suburbs fill up—and they will eventually—cottages might be built on eighty-foot-wide platforms over streets. The concept is not as outrageous as it may seem. In Europe and Asia bridges lined with stores and houses are not uncommon (the Ponte Vecchio in Florence is probably the most famous example). Overpasses, both pedestrian and vehicular, span American highways, and in New York and other cities apartment and office buildings have been built over major thoroughfares. Construction over busy highways might not be a good idea because of the pollution and noise, but pollution and noise are not significant problems for less-traveled and quieter streets in suburban neighborhoods, or for back roads on the outskirts. To provide clearance for trucks and fire engines, the streets would have to be lowered five feet below grade and the platforms built seven feet above ground level, giving an overall clearance of twelve feet. Planters and perhaps grass turf in setting beds could be used for landscaping. I envisage that in the not-too-distant future cities and their suburbs will merge contiguously with underutilized suburban infill sites, abandoned military sites, light-industrial sites, and old school lands to create high-density residential areas that are close to work and shopping centers, taking advantage of existing infrastructure. The result would be a substantial environmental victory—a major reduction in air pollution and automobile use and the creation of green and healthy home spaces.

With good public transportation, intermittent parks, and careful planning to ensure a residential/commercial/industrial balance, we can provide comfortable housing for everyone in a salubrious environment. The alternative is bleak: more homelessness and further destruction of the environment.

Chapter Eight

DESIGN FOR CHANGE

An innovation's ultimate contribution is not simply that it meets some need more effectively, but that it alters a socially constructed sense of reality and broadens it to accept new forms of action and thought.

Allan D. Wallis[1]

A SEED IS PLANTED

The idea of a convertible residential space was born during a discussion between me and Walter Harrington, a partner and developer of the Two Worlds concept in Mountain View, California. He and I noted the amount of unsold, high-priced, large three-, four-, and five-bedroom houses in a small upper-middle-income California city. We reckoned that if the developer of the houses could break each house into two, three, or four units he could then sell the units in an affordable cost range and thereby rid himself of his debt and give the community an affordable housing resource. The flexibility allowing an owner to change housing stock to follow market needs has never really been adequately explored by the industry. The idea that a developer should be able to adjust his product, after it has been built, to the needs of potential buyers is the basis for developing the following convertible house.

MacDonald Architects began with a convertible space for residential townhouses. Ever receptive to innovation, Harrington and Kulakoff liked the concept and had us draw preliminary designs for a kit of parts to be used in the construction of townhouses to be built in Menlo Park, California. The convertible townhouse could be rented or sold as a single two-story unit or it could be divided into two separate units.

Prospective residents would choose what plan they wanted while the project was under construction. If a family wanted both floors, they would have a spacious three-bedroom, three-bath home. If divided, the dining room on the first floor would be converted into a bedroom. The master bedroom on the second floor would become a living room and the second bathroom a kitchen. At a later time the two units could be easily reconverted into a townhouse, or vice versa. Thus the demand really determined the supply. What people wanted and could afford, they could have.

Unfortunately, the project was not built due to city government's lack of interest in the housing needs of the community's middle- and low-income classes, and the inflexible regulations: more on-site parking would be required if a townhouse was divided into two units; the enlarged parking need was too much for the site. But the concept of a convertible home, whether a townhouse, a regular detached house, or an apartment, nagged at me. I wanted to carry it further, to a design that would enable people to easily adapt their homes as their needs and financial condition changed over the years.

CONVERTIBLE HOMES

A basic attribute of our political system is the ability to effect change peacefully—in one's personal life and in the government. Americans are apt to forget how rare that ability is in the world. They change jobs, move about the country, install and remove officials, start new businesses, go bankrupt, and reinvent themselves continually. Traditional architecture has never reflected that empowerment of the people. It has always stressed permanence, finality. "Great buildings last forever" is a common belief, and we look in wonderment at the Medici Palace, Versailles, the White House, and the other homes of the mighty of the world. People's homes should not be permanent and final. They they should be flexible, they should be changeable, they should express freedom of choice. The cottages I designed, with their twin capabilities of expansion and individualization, express this spirit. Convertible homes would be another way to enable people to control their living environment and allow them to remain in the same house and neighborhood through their lifetimes.

Upper Level

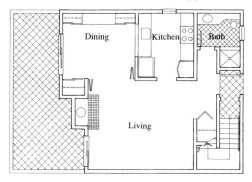

Lower Level

On the first level of the townhouse, the entry door is on the right-hand side, adjacent to the stairway to the second level. On the left-hand side next to the living room is the private outdoor yard. On the left-hand side of the second floor is the outdoor deck with a waist-high planter around its edge. This planter and the main bedroom sliding glass doors create an exterior privacy zone for the occupant.

Setting flexibility as a primary goal, I developed a design for Harrington-Kulakoff that would make it possible for residents of a townhouse to convert it into two flats in a matter of four hours—and back again in the same amount of time. (The method would be applicable to a regular detached house, of course, but at the time I was thinking in terms of mixed-use or multiunit projects.) Considering the townhouse—or house—as a lifetime investment, a young couple could rent out the lower flat to pay the mortgage, then when children came, occupy the entire house, and when they retired, rent or sell the upper story to supplement their income. Or the owner could rent or sell it as a single unit or two apartments, whichever was most advantageous in the market at the time.

The first floor of the townhouse consists of a living room, dining room, kitchen, and bath, with a patio on the side. Upstairs are two bedrooms and two baths, with a balcony off the master bedroom. In four hours or less, the house can be converted into two one-bedroom flats simply by moving and installing elements of what I call, for lack of a better term, the "quick-change kit," which is stored in the house.

Before   Lower Level

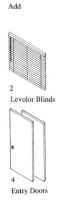

After   Lower Flat

Delete

1
Entry Door

Add

2
Levolor Blinds

3
Washer / Dryer

4
Entry Doors

Lower-level floor plan before and after conversion. The items shown on the right are to be removed or added to make the conversion.

Starting with the first floor, you move the entry door from the outside to the inside of the vestibule and install a second door near the foot of the staircase to the second floor. The hinges are in place and the second door has been stored ready for use under the staircase, so the whole process should take no more than ten minutes. (As an alternative, the outside door might be left where it is and two doors added to create a closed vestibule. That, of course, would require the purchase of an extra door, but it would be a shelf item obtainable at any building-materials store.) The dining room is instantly converted into a bedroom by pulling down a Murphy bed installed in the wall and closing the accordion doors across the kitchen serving shelf.

Conversion of the second floor is a little more complicated, but not much. To change the master bedroom into a living-dining room, just roll away the two clothes racks that were in the dressing alcove, which is large enough to hold a dining table. It is the conversion of the master bathroom into a kitchen that takes some doing. First, remove the toilet, shower door, and mirror, and place a platform over the shower base. The platform, a refrigera-

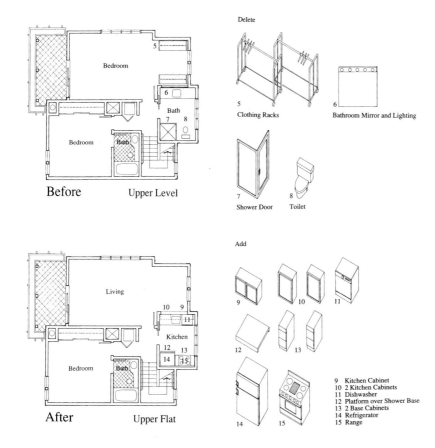

Upper-level floor plan before and after conversion. The items shown on the right are to be removed or added to make the conversion.

tor, a stove, and a dishwasher have been stored next to the closet in the small bedroom from the time of the house's completion. Move the appliances into the kitchen, placing the refrigerator where the shower used to be, the stove centered over the toilet drain, and the dishwasher in the corner next to the sink. (Large appliances are all equipped with rollers.) The necessary electrical outlets have already been installed, and the dishwasher is the movable type with hoses that can be connected to the water spout at the sink. Hang cabinets (stored under the stairs) on hooks provided on the wall. That's it. The only tools needed for the entire conversion are a wrench, a hammer, and a sturdy screwdriver for use in knocking the pins out of the door hinges.

DO-IT-YOURSELF APARTMENTS

Because one problem leads to another, I continued to puzzle over ways to make apartments more flexible. Why should people have

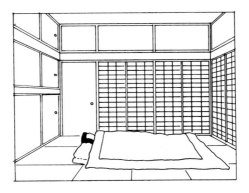

Flexible room in a traditional Japanese modular home. It is used here to demonstrate the multiple use of one space and its conversion from a dining room to a bedroom. Below, the sliding doors are shown open to create a living-dining space. Note that the furniture used in this space is modular and easily stored.

to settle for a fixed layout? Why not let them create their own living space?

My first idea was to adapt to Western apartment living the movable partitions, folding screens, and built-in wall cabinets of the conventional Japanese house. The Japanese architect Koji Yagi[2] has written a fascinating book full of excellent ideas for modifications of houses, and some are certainly applicable to apartments. As he points out, a Japanese room ordinarily has several functions, which change in the course of a day and from day to day. It might serve as a living room, a dining room, and at night a bedroom. By opening and closing sliding partitions the size of the room can be expanded or contracted as needed—usage determines space.

Screens can be used to divide the space further. Furniture, linens, and futons for sleeping are kept in modular wall cabinets, from which they are removed when needed and to which they are promptly returned when not, most Japanese residential furniture being minimal and portable.

Actually, sliding doors used to be commonplace in the design of late-nineteenth-century American apartments, particularly between the living room and dining room, but also between all the rooms in so-called railroad flats. Since there were few, if any, closets and built-in cabinets, clothes were hung in wardrobes, bed linens and extra blankets were stored in chests of drawers, dining linens and utensils were kept in sideboards and dishes in highboys or the like. Although the pieces were usually very large, and once in place along the walls might remain there for decades, they could be moved if need be.

The use of the sliding partition was therefore an obvious solution to the problem of how to create more flexible space. But it was far from satisfactory. It was in place, and could only be moved back and forth along one line. Sliding partitions expanded and contracted space; they didn't really change it. Folding screens were better. But that left the problem of furniture. Westerners were not going to be content with sleeping on futons, sitting on tiny floor-level chairs, and eating on low tables. Wherever the bed was placed, that would be the bedroom; wherever the sofa was, that would be the living room. So in the final analysis the screens, like the partitions, would only contract or expand space, not reshape it.

Then I came up with another idea. It derived to a certain extent from artists' studios I had visited when I was a graduate student in New York. They were lofts, usually on the top floor of old light-industry buildings in lower Manhattan, and had large windows. The artist would use most of the space for his work, but might divide off part with an old-fashioned wardrobe, high bookcases, and storage cabinets to create a private bedroom. There was nothing unique or especially interesting about the use of furniture as room dividers, but it did convey the feeling that the artist possessed the space, that the space was all his to shape

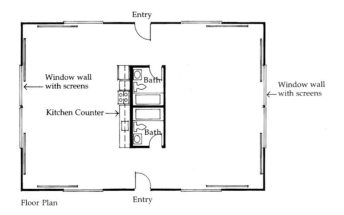

Floor Plan

A volume has been sized to provide flexible and affordable living accommodations. The central internal wall contains all the utilities except the electrical lines, which would be distributed throughout the perimeter walls. The permanently fixed central core (kitchen and bathrooms) is surrounded by a perimeter wall that can be changed to any desired form.

A storage closet is made up of $^3/_4$-inch plywood. This cabinet sits on a base that has recessed casters so it can be rolled into different positions depending on intended use.

A sliding panel can be applied to the back of cabinets in locations where a privacy door is needed.

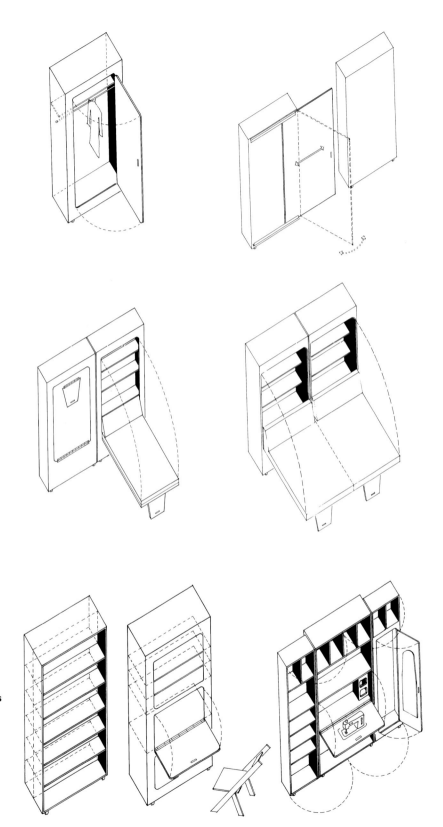

Cabinet for a fold-down single or double bed. These movable elements have the bedding attached to the front panel. The shelving behind the bed can be used for storage of books or other items.

A double-sided bookcase can be rolled on casters throughout the interior.

Combined cabinet with a pull-down desktop and shelves for storage above and below.

This sewing center contains storage areas for clothes to be mended and ironed. The center has a flip-top desk surface on which a sewing machine is mounted. On the right-hand side of the drawing is a panel that swings out. An ironing board is stored inside.

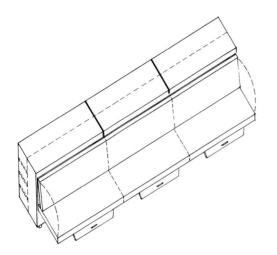
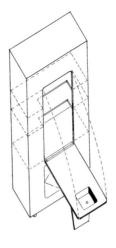
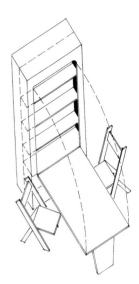

and allot as he wanted to, and that as a result it was an integral part of his life, instead of an enclosure he occupied.

With the image of a loft in mind, I designed a hypothetical 32- x 48-foot envelope with window walls and entrances. This envelope can be changed, taking on different forms, such as a circle, a square, or a curvilinear wall. The only permanent division of the internal space is a wet core consisting of two adjacent bathrooms and an open kitchen counter with sink and electrical and plumbing outlets for appliances. Power strips along the walls and outlets in the floor enable the occupants to plug in lamps and whatnot almost anywhere.

Many pieces of furniture are built into a cabinet on recessed casters, with dimensions two feet by four feet by seve feet, eleven inches high—an adaptation of the immense movable closets and cabinets found in old apartments. It can be rolled around under the eight-foot ceiling, but effectively serves as a space divider since there's only one-half inch of space between the bottom and the floor and the top and the ceiling. Cabinets can be attached to form a wall, and they have sliding panels in back that can be used as doors or wall extensions. When fully open the panels pivot, so that walls can be extended at angles as well as horizontally.

For example, to create a bedroom: one cabinet contains a single bed, which is lowered like a Murphy bed. Another contains shelves, and yet another serves as a desk. A chair might be added, and a desk, and perhaps a sewing center in an alcove.

The bedroom might be positioned next to one of the bathrooms and extended with cabinets and panels to a windowed wall. For the living room, three cabinets containing easy chairs

Three low cabinets can either be placed together as a sofa or separated as lounge seats. Each seating section has a bookshelf in the back.

The bar cabinet shows the open counter with a sink and shelving for glasses and bottles. A bucket should be placed under the sink drain.

An in-place dining table panel swings down from its vertical position to rest on a pivoting leg. The shelving in this cabinet will be used to store dishes, silverware, linens, and other items related to dining.

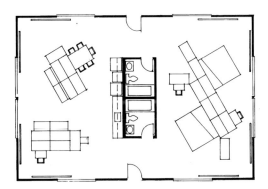

Below is one possible layout of a do-it-yourself aptartment. The sleeping area shows two queen-size beds and a sleeping area divided by high cabinets. The remaining space shows a dining area for five people and a living area with four lounging/sofa modules. Above is the same space, but with rearranged sleeping and dining areas.

might be combined to form a couch with bookshelves on the back. Another has bookshelves, another opens up into a bar, another contains stacked side tables with reading lamps. All items needed for dining—a table, chairs, linens, dishes, silverware—are included in another one. Voila! A completely furnished apartment.

If you are tired of the layout and want to rearrange the apartment, perhaps with a second bedroom, you can do it in less than half an hour.

HOMES ON WHEELS

While the convertible house and do-it-yourself apartment are much more flexible than conventional homes, the freedom they afford is limited. However changeable the interiors might be, these homes are rooted in place, tied to the umbilical cord of utilities, and confined by four external walls; they are, moreover, permanently destructive of the land on which they are built. The alternative is evident on American highways: mobile homes of one type or another—from luxurious motorized vehicles the size of a small house (and costing as much as a house) to campers fitted onto a pickup truck to curtained vans with sleeping bags strewn on the floor and old buses with their windows boarded up and seats pulled out to make way for beds. Most are simply holiday cottages on wheels, and for getting away from it all there's nothing quite like them. The sense of independence is incomparable. You can go where you want, when you want to, changing your environment as you please, seeking new experience. In the United States especially, but increasingly in other countries as well, you can find gas stations, convenience stores, restaurants, and places to stop along the way almost anywhere. The existing national highway grid, with its supporting facilities in place, makes the nomadic life possible.

The motorized mobile home (as distinguished from the trailer home found in trailer parks) can also be a long-term or permanent dwelling, however, and that function has been neglected for the most part except for the luxurious models. There are many people who by necessity, or choice, are nomads. In some cases they are obliged to move from place to place because their jobs require it—salesmen, for example, construction workers, certain specialized engineers, musicians (it was youthful rock-and-roll groups in the 1960s who got the idea of buying old buses for the travels from gig to gig). They might have a permanent home, but spend a great deal of their time on the road. In times of high unemployment blue-collar workers sometimes have to leave their families behind while they search the country for jobs and may have to live away for long periods when they find one. And then there are those who love to wander, who travel from place to place picking up odd jobs, and those who have saved some money and want to spend it seeing the world. A number of companies have designed large recreational vehicles that would be ideal for such nomads.

For example, the sleek and highly efficient Legacy Motorhome built by Airstream contains everything needed for a comfortable life on wheels, including a bedroom, a bathroom with toilet and shower, a kitchen, and a lounge that can be converted into a second bedroom.

Utility systems are built in: a generator for lights and heat, freshwater and wastewater tanks, vacuum system, radio-telephone and propane gas for the stove, water heater, and operation of the generator. Because the utility system is internalized in the vehicle, the overall consumption of energy and resources is less than it would be in a conventional home, despite the motor-

The van is one of my first designs for an affordable cottage on wheels. The interior cabinet system of doors and shelves is built of ³/₄-inch plywood. The utility pieces such as stove, sink, water tank, toilet, and heater are camping items that can be readily obtained from catalogs.

home's gas consumption while traveling. Centralized "stations" with utilities in-place could also be shared by motorhomes when required. This would take advantage of existing infrastructure and free the land from further encroachment.

The Legacy Motorhome is furnished like a conventional home, with a sofa, easy chairs, a dinette set, a queen-size bed, and such amenities as a television, AM/FM/CD player with power amplifier, and even a coffee maker. However, it is expensive and intended primarily for family vacations and for retirees who like to take long trips. No suitable motorized mobile home has been built for occupancy by people with low incomes. I decided to design one.

The question was how to fit into an affordable vehicle the systems and basic furnishings needed for a self-contained home. It would have to include water, cooking facilities, light, and heat, along with a bed, chairs, a table, and storage space. In addition, I wanted the "cottage on wheels" to be capable of doubling as a business vehicle, so it could be used for deliveries or carrying tools during the week and for recreation on weekends. Nomads could earn some money performing odd jobs as they traveled, or itinerant craftsmen might use it as a shop for selling their wares. The more flexible the mobile home, the better it would be.

My obvious choice for a vehicle was therefore a van. My design concept was to use camping equipment for the utility systems, and to tuck them all way in storage cabinets along the interior walls when the van was rolling.

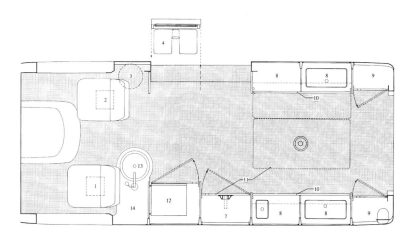

1 DRIVERS SEAT
2 PASSENGER SEAT
3 FUEL-STORAGE FOR COOK-STOVE
4 FOLDING TABLE FOR COOK-
  STOVE, ATTACHED TO DOOR
5 STORAGE, KITCHEN EQUIPMENT
6 FOOD STORAGE
7 CLOTH STORAGE
8 STORAGE

9 STORAGE, CLEANING EQUIPMENT
10 PANEL, FOLDABLE TO SERVE AS
   SEAT OR PART OF BED PLATFORM
11 PANEL WITH TUBE RECEPTACLE
   TO SERVE AS TABLE TOP OR BED
   PLATFORM
12 2.5 CUBIC FEET ICE-BOX
13 SINK WITH HAND-PUMP FAUCET
14 COUNTERTOP

The floor plan of the van shows the areas of multiple use for washing, cooking, eating, and sleeping. The driver's seat is in the lower left-hand corner.

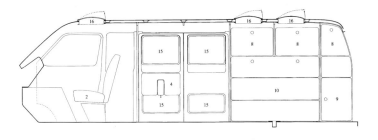

Cross sections through the van show the ³/₄-inch ply-wood panelized wall system in elevation and in a closed position for use as a delivery van.

1 DRIVERS SEAT
2 PASSENGER SEAT
3 FUEL-STORAGE FOR COOK-STOVE
4 FOLDING TABLE FOR COOK-
   STOVE, ATTACHED TO DOOR
5 STORAGE, KITCHEN EQUIPMENT
6 FOOD STORAGE
7 CLOTH STORAGE
8 STORAGE
9 STORAGE, CLEANING EQUIPMENT
10 PANEL, FOLDABLE TO SERVE AS
   SEAT OR PART OF BED PLATFORM
11 PANEL WITH TUBE RECEPTACLE
   TO SERVE AS TABLE TOP OR BED
   PLATFORM
12 2.5 CUBIC FEET ICE-BOX
13 SINK WITH HAND-PUMP FAUCET
14 COUNTERTOP
15 WINDOW
16 14" x 24" OPERABLE SKYLIGHT

View from open rear door of the van, looking at the movable double bed platform.

The basic systems include:

Propane stove
Sink with hand pump
Freshwater tank
Wastewater tank
Portable chemical toilet
Catalytic heaters

Also provided are such amenities of modern life as a 2.5-cubic-foot ice chest, electric lamps, a battery-operated television, and a battery-operated radio/stereo system. Three fourteen-inch by twenty-four-inch operable skylights are inserted in the ceilings.

When the van is in use for business, or while traveling, all the systems are stored in cabinets or hidden behind panels. There are also closets for storing food, clothing, utensils, and the like. All the doors to the compartments and panels are made of plywood. At night you can easily transform the van into a bedroom. You lower the hinged doors of two cabinets (number eight on the floor plan) and lock them into the van's floor, forming the head and foot of a double bed. Remove the door of the storage cabinet for clothing (number seven on the floor plan) and place it between the head and foot panels.

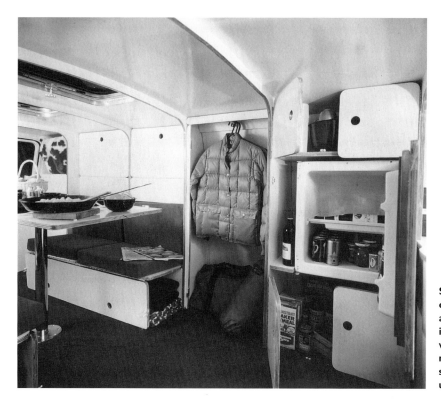

Sleeping area at the back of the van transformed into a dining space. This change is made by taking the plywood panel that was originally covering the clothing storage compartment and using it as a table top.

A foam mattress and linens are kept in the cabinets above the bed. For dining, raise the center bed panel. It forms a table and the head and foot panels become benches. Remove the doors covering the ice chest and sink, and place the propane stove on the hinged shelf attached to one of the van's side doors. A shelf on the other side door is for cooking utensils. If you prefer to dine al fresco, you can use the roof as a deck or you can attach an awning to hooks provided on the side of the van. Indeed, awnings can be attached to both sides and the rear to expand the living space if you plan to stay at one location for a while. Like the basic cottage, the cottage on wheels becomes an armature.

DEMOCRACY AND THE NOMADIC LIFE

Europeans and their New World descendants have generally considered nomadism to be a primitive way of life, often viewing it with suspicion and malice. The Gypsies, those great wanderers of mysterious origin, have been maligned and persecuted to the point that half a million were murdered by the Nazis in concentration camps. Vagabonds and hoboes are harassed, jailed, and driven from town. Young people traveling in their vans and boarded-up buses can count on being stopped time and again by the police.

Behind the antagonism is an ingrained intolerance of the free spirit, of people who choose to live outside the social grid however peaceful and law-abiding they may be. It is a frighteningly undemocratic mentality, and even in a relatively free society like the United States there is evidence of a disposition toward totalitarianism. A person who is rooted in one place, preferably owning property, is thought to be controllable and willing to be controlled. That person is seen as no threat to the established social order. But the wanderer sees many things and becomes tolerant and flexible. The wanderer does not dig up the land, or destroy forests, or divert waterways, but adapts to the environment. If welcomed, the wanderer can be a source of information and new ideas. We should encourage nomads by creating a network of the facilities they need when they pause along the way.

Ironically, the kind of mobile society I'm thinking of is represented by the truckers who ply the roads of rural Pakistan, carrying manufactured goods from the cities to the villages and village crafts back to the urbanites.[3] The driver and his assistants live in the truck while they're on the road, which for the driver at least is almost all the time, although he might have a family housed in a village. A typical truck consists of a bare chassis on which a body has been built by a local workshop out of wood slats and metal and wood crosspieces in accordance with government regulations with due regard for variations requested by the owner. It might contain secret storage areas or windows of a certain size, for example. Then the truck receives its "identity." Painters decorate it with signs, symbols, and motifs under the owner's or driver's direction. It becomes an expression of the trucker's personality, or in any case the way he wants to be seen by the world. (Rural buses are similarly decorated.)

Over the years a network of elaborate truck stops has sprung up along arteries and near terminals in the cities. Called *addas,* they include workshops for repair and maintenance of the trucks and, most important for the truckers, a tea shop, where they can get together to talk and have a bite to eat, write letters or have them written by scribes, or just read the newspaper. The addas are modern versions of the caravansary.

Although there are plenty of truck stops in the United States and many campsites for recreational vehicles, there are no caravansaries where the wanderers can stay awhile, have their vehicles repaired, and take care of their personal needs. That the demand for such facilities exists is attested by the number of curtained vans and cars one sees parked in city streets and on the side of country roads at night. In many cases their occupants are homeless, some are genuine nomads, but often they are people with homes who are looking for jobs. We are probably going to see a lot more of the last group, the job seekers, in the future. The trend is for companies to trim down their work forces, to hire people when needed and then lay them off when their services are no longer required. Technological companies, especially, sometimes require people for specific projects and depend, or would like to be able to depend, on a pool of workers with the appropriate skills who are available for short periods.

We may indeed be returning in a sense to the preindustrial era of the skilled craftsman, and that might not be a bad thing. More flexible types of industrial organization and social relationships might develop. Fixed communities would exercise less control, people would be less regulated, less fearful of losing jobs, less tied to property and possessions. They would be more free to order their own lives. And any way that individual freedom can be enhanced is worthy.

A CALL TO ACTION

In the last decade of the twentieth century, the globalization of our economy and the spread of unregulated capitalism to formerly communist nations indicate a change in social thinking. One of the outcomes will be a decrease in public funding of lower-income housing. Consequently, the need for new housing solutions here and abroad will be great. The United Nations' *Global Report on Human Settlements: An Urbanizing World* sums up the coming housing crisis: "The bottom line is that the 21st century will be the first urban century. The problem is that we are woefully unprepared for it." In the United States the public's cry for a balanced federal budget will undoubtedly cause public housing funds to be closely scrutinized. The likely cutbacks will be felt in all forms of public housing and in maintenance budgets for existing government-owned housing stock, as well as by non-profit developers relying on subsidized housing tax-credit bonds for the construction of non-profit housing.

The fact is that our government has done a poor job of providing adequate housing for its people. Up to forty percent of our population is deprived of a decent home, with many families crammed in single rooms or sleeping in shelters and on the streets. Yet far less wealthy countries like Holland, Sweden, Denmark, Norway, Finland, Germany, France, Canada, and even England, with its battered economy, have managed to more effectively address the housing needs of their lower-income citizens. I wrote *Democratic Architecture* to inspire those in our country's private and public sectors to build safe, comfortable, and affordable homes for *all* people. Building professionals should make a commitment to study, advocate, and address our ever-changing need for housing. Otherwise, we abandon that forty percent that needs our creative design and problem-solving talents the most.

This book provides real and workable examples of affordable construction, achieved with or without government funding and suitable for a multiplicity of lifestyles and budgets. In some cases, those with elementary carpentry skills will find that they can build some of these structures themselves with surprisingly little time and money. And the prototypes of mobile homes and shelters featured in these pages merely hint at what we can do to create secure environments for people at even the lowest levels of the economic scale.

For years faceless politicians have obstructed the creation of better housing to appease wealthier homeowners concerned with possible decreases in property values. By prolonging the development permit process, manipulating regulations, and wielding political pressure, the obstructionists have been especially destructive in areas of suburban and urban infill, mobile housing sites, and mixed-income neighborhoods. Building accessibly priced homes—from a minimal city sleeper for a homeless person to a high-density urban infill residential unit—is of the highest priority, and should not be left up to bureaucrats but put into the hands of the people. It is my hope that this book will help generate that sea change.

NOTES

INTRODUCTION

1. According to one report, "Nearly 27 million households in the United States—containing 78 million people, or 32 percent of the population—face so great a squeeze between adequate incomes and high housing costs that, after paying for their housing, they are unable to meet their non-shelter needs at even a minimum level of adequacy." Michael E. Stone, *One-Third of a Nation* (Washington: Economic Policy Institute, 1990), p. 1.

2. Jane Jacobs, *The Death and Life of Great American Cities* (New York: Vintage Books, 1961), p. 45.

CHAPTER I

1. Robert Sommer, *Tight Spaces: Hard Architecture and How to Humanize It* (Englewood Cliffs, N.J.: Prentice-Hall, Inc., 1974), p. 2.

2. Ibid., p. v.

3. Daniel J. Boorstin, *The Americans: The Democratic Experience* (New York: Random House, 1973), p. 290.

4. Richard Plunz, *A History of Housing in New York City* (New York: Columbia University Press, 1990), pp. 330-334.

5. Robert Gifford, *Environmental Psychology: Principles and Practice* (Boston: Allyn Bacon, Inc., 1987), pp. 210, 219-220.

6. Oscar Newman, *Defensible Space* (New York: Collier Books, 1973), p. 4.

7. Quoted in Bruce Brooks Pfeiffer and Gerald Nordland (eds.), *Frank Lloyd Wright in the Realm of Ideas* (Carbondale and Edwardsville: Southern Illinois University Press), p. 72.

8. Real Estate Research Corporation, *The Costs of Sprawl* (Washington, D.C.: U.S. Government Printing Office, April 1974), Executive Summary, p. 1. The report was prepared for Council of Environmental Quality, Department of Housing and Urban Development, and the Environmental Protection Agency. For the purposes of the study, prototypes were developed of different communities, each consisting of 10,000 dwelling units on 6000 acres of land. *Low-density sprawl* was defined as an entire community "made up of single family homes, seventy-five percent sited in a traditional grid pattern and the rest clustered.

Neighborhoods are sited in a 'leapfrog' pattern with little contiguity. This represents the typical pattern of suburban development." *High density* was defined as a planned ("meaning general compactness of development") community in which "housing is composed of forty percent high rise apartments, thirty percent walkup apartments, twenty percent townhouses, and ten percent clustered single family homes. All of the dwelling units are clustered together in contiguous neighborhoods, much in a pattern of a high density 'new community'" (Executive Summary, p. 2). Prototypes of four other communities were also studied.

CHAPTER 2

1. Bruno Zevi (1918-), professor of architectural history at the University of Rome and editor of *L'Architectura* (Rome), is the author of numerous books, including *The Modern Language of Architecture*, published by University of Washington Press (1978).

2. Le Corbusier, *The Radiant City*, translated by Pamela Knight, Eleanor Levieux, Derek Coleman (New York: The Orion Press, 1967), p. 144.

3. Op. cit., p. 146.

4. Ibid.

5. Bruno Zevi, *The Modern Language of Architecture* (Seattle and London: University of Washington Press, 1978), p. 32.

6. For a fascinating discussion of mail-order homes, see Alan Gowans. *The Comfortable Home: North American Suburban Architecture 1890-1930* (Cambridge, MA, and London: The MIT Press, 1986), pp. 41-67.

7. They probably included the poet-philosopher Ralph Waldo Emerson, the educator Amos Bronson Alcott, and the theologian William Ellery Channing—hardly professional construction workers.

8. Henry David Thoreau, *The Variorum Walden and the Variorum Civil Disobedience* (New York: Washington Square Press, 1968), pp. 32-35.

9. Philip Langdon, *American Houses* (New York: Stewart, Tabori & Chang, 1987), p. 137.

10. Hassan Fathy, *Architecture for the Poor* (Cairo: The American University in Cairo Press, 1989), p. 45.

11. Ibid., pp. 54, 58.

12. Ibid., p. 54.

13. Zvi Hecker, "Israeli Art and Islamic Culture," pp.1-3.

CHAPTER 4

1. Hassan Fathy (1900-) has taught at the Faculty of Fine Arts in Cairo University and served as head of its Department of Architecture. He received the Agfa Khan Award for Architecture in 1980 and the Union of International Architects Gold Medal in 1984. He is also the founder and director of the International Institute for Appropriate Technology. His now classic work, *Architecture for the Poor*, was published by the American University of Cairo Press in 1973.

2. Jan Zovickian, "A Day in the Life," *Fog Cutter* (December 12, 1989), p. 4.

3. *Beyond Shelter: A Homeless Plan for San Francisco. A Statement of Need* (November 1990), p. 1.

4. Ibid., p. 29.

5. Ibid., p. 53.

6. For a discussion of the differences between the occupants of the old skid rows and the current homeless, see Peter H. Rossi, "The Old Homeless and the New Homelessness in Historical Perspective," *American Psychologist* (August 1990), pp. 954-959.

7. *San Francisco Chronicle,* [Donald: Page number and date?]

8. Quoted in *San Francisco Examiner,* March 20, 1988, p. A5.

CHAPTER 5

1. Lewis Mumford, *Architecture as a Home for Man* (New York: Architectural Record Books, 1975), pp. 150, 153.

2. Jacobs, op. cit., p. 15.

3. The project was developed jointly by East Bay Asian Local Development Corporation (EBALDC) and BRIDGE Housing Corporation. The financing included a $5,524,000 Housing Development Action Grant from the Department of Housing and Urban Development, a $4 million deferred payment loan from the Redevelopment Agency of the City of Oakland, a $500,000 grant from the Department of Health and Human Services, a payment by the Oakland Public Works Department for development of underground parking facilities to be owned by the city, a $416,500 interest subsidy from the Federal Home Loan Bank of San Francisco, and loans by Wells Fargo Bank and Citibank.

4. Under Section 8 of the Housing Act of 1974 the federal government pays a portion of the rent for certain low-income families and single persons over sixty-two years of age—so-called Section 8 Certificate holders.

5. Herb Childress, "In Living Context," *Express* (March 8, 1991), pp. 13-14.

CHAPTER 6

1. Daniel Solomon, *Rebuilding* (New York: Princeton Architectural Press, 1992), p. 37.

2. City and County of San Francisco, Department of City Planning, Richmond Square, Preliminary Draft, Environmental Impact Report Draft II (March 12, 1991), p. 3.

3. John Holtzclaw, "Efficient Transportation—For the Earth's Sake," Statement to the Senate Banking, Housing and Urban Affairs Committee, August 8, 1990. The mortality statistic was from a 1980 study by the Harvard School of Public Health and the health-care and work-loss statistic from a report by the American Lung Association.

4. John Holtzclaw, "Explaining Urban Density and Transit Impacts on Auto Use," Report by the Natural Resources Defense Council and The Sierra Club to the State of California Energy Resources Conservation and Development Commission, January 15, 1991.

CHAPTER 7

1. Greenbelt Alliance, *Reviving the Sustainable Metropolis,* p. 14.

2. For discussions of Seaside, see *Progressive Architecture* (July 1985), pp. 110-119; Kelher Ann Easterling, "Public Enterprise," *Landscape*

(1985), pp. 35-43; Andres Duany and Elizabeth Plater-Zyberk, "The Town of Seaside," ibid., pp. 44-50.

    3. F.A.I.A.—Fellow of the American Institute of Architects. The fellowship is conferred to an architect by his peers in recognition of extraordinary achievement and contribution to architecture.

    4. John Field, "Seaside Broadside," *Architecture California* (November 1992), p. 45.

    5. Vincent Scully, *Pueblo Mountain, Village, Dance* (New York: The Viking Press, 1975), pp. 58-61.

    6. The term "heritage trees" is used by planning departments to describe existing large trees that cannot be cut down to make way for a project.

CHAPTER 8

    1. Alan D. Wallis, *Wheel Estate* (New York and Oxford: Oxford University Press, 1991), p. 254.

    2. Koji Yagi, *A Japanese Touch for Your Home* (Tokyo, New York, San Francisco: Kodansha International Ltd., 1982).

    3. Hasan-Uddin Khan, "Mobile Shelter in Pakistan," in Paul Oliver (ed.), *Shelter, Sign & Symbol* (Woodstock, New York: The Overlook Press, 1977), pp. 183-96.

INDEX

PHOTOGRAPHY CREDITS